5   10 m

LOG HOUSES
OF THE WORLD

Richard Olsen

PHOTOGRAPHY BY **Radek Kurzaj**

WITH DRAWINGS BY DAVID PERRELLI

ABRAMS : NEW YORK

CONTENTS

INTRODUCTION 6

SOME PROTOTYPES 12

THE LOG HOUSE AND THE WORLD'S FAIRS 16

The Tour

1890 Frögnerseteren
Holm Hansen Munthe, Architect. Oslo, Norway 24

1893 Ravine Lodge
William W. Boyington, Architect. Highland Park, Illinois 30

1897 Dom Pod Jedlami
Stanislaw Witkiewicz, Architect. Zakopane, Poland 40

1903 Hvitträsk
Herman Gesellius, Armas Lindgren, and Eliel Saarinen Architects.
Kirkkonummi, Finland 48

1904–06 Tallom
Lars Israel Wahlman, Architect. Stocksund, Sweden 56

1911 Clubhouse, Stickley Museum at Craftsman Farms
Gustav Stickley, Designer. Morris Plains, New Jersey 64

1913 Power House
Robert C. Reamer and William E. Donovan, Architects. Wolf Creek, Montana 72

1913 Semmering House
Adolf Loos, Architect. Semmering, Austria 80

1916–18 Log House
R. M. Schindler, Architect. Location Unknown 84

1924 Villa Vekara
Alvar Aalto, Architect. Karstula, Finland 88

1924 Hellman House
Alfred Heineman, Designer. Santa Monica, California 92

1930–33 The Point (formerly Camp Wonundra)
William Distin, Architect. Upper Saranac Lake, New York 100

1951 Helburn House
Richard Neutra, Architect. Bozeman, Montana 108

1952 Le Petit Cabanon
Le Corbusier, Architect. Roquebrune-Cap-Martin, France 116

1957 Pearlman Cabin
John Lautner, Architect. Idyllwild, California 124

1959–63 Terry House
Roland Terry, Architect. Lopez Island, Washington 130

1966–80 **Brekkestranda Fjord Hotel**
Bjorn Simonnaes, Architect. Brekke, Norway   *138*

1993 **Koether House**
Katharina Kölbel, Architect. Stetten, Germany   *144*

1993 **Ashley House**
David Ashley, Architect. Gold Hill, Colorado   *150*

1993 **Neiman Guest House**
David Neiman, Architect. Deming, Washington   *156*

1994 **Gugalun**
Peter Zumthor, Restoration/Addition Architect. Versam, Switzerland   *162*

1998 **Tunebjer House "Vistet"**
Anders Landström and Thomas Sandell, Architects. Torö, Sweden   *168*

1999 **Heavenly View Ranch**
Robert A. M. Stern, Architect. Snowmass, Colorado   *176*

2000 **Zajac House**
Sebastian Piton, Architect. Zakopane, Poland   *182*

2003 **Midnight Canyon Ranch**
Kelly F. Faloon, Architect. Montana   *188*

2003 **Lanzinger House**
Antonius Lanzinger, Architect. Brixlegg, Austria   *196*

2003 **Savage House**
Kurt Dubbe, Architect. Driggs, Idaho   *202*

2004 **Orcas House**
Mira Jean Steinbrecher, Architect. Orcas Island, Washington   *210*

2004 **Draper Cabin**
Daniel Vincent Scully, Architect. Hancock, New Hampshire   *218*

LOG JOINERY TYPES   228

NOTES   230

BIBLIOGRAPHY   234

INDEX   236

AUTHOR'S ACKNOWLEDGMENTS   240

ABOVE Waterfront-elevation drawing of Brekkestranda Fjord Hotel in Brekke, Norway, prepared in 1966 by architect Bjorn Simonnaes. Simonnaes, now age 84, resides in Bergen, Norway. In the city's phone directory he lists himself as "Nest Builder."

PAGE 1 Drawing detail of the front elevation of Frögnerseteren in Oslo, Norway, prepared about 1890 by architect Holm Hansen Munthe.

Although it does not figure prominently in the collective imagination of Americans, there is such a thing as the high-art log house. In the United States, we cherish the log cabin as an emblem of the country's humble beginnings, and for a nation that has often struggled to find its history, the log cabin is our rock. That heavily mythologized image of the uncivilized pioneer who labors to stake his claim on the wide-open frontier is one we often turn to in search of our national identity.

The log cabin is also a political emblem, representing the modest but somehow alluring origin of many of our early presidents, including Andrew Jackson (1767–1845); James Buchanan (1791–1868); and the most widely known, Abraham Lincoln (1809–1865). As historian Richard Guy Wilson points out, there was a period in our nation's history when "one couldn't get elected president without a log cabin in his past."[1] In the identity of the gay-rights political group known as the Log Cabin Republicans, we see that politics and the image of the log cabin have become close relatives.

The image of the log cabin is also inseparable from that of a well-known traditional children's toy. Since 1916, when John Lloyd Wright, son of architect Frank Lloyd Wright, first introduced his invention Lincoln Logs, the miniature-log construction set has gone on to sell more than one hundred million sets worldwide.[2] Originally made of real redwood, Wright's toy was conceived as a way to teach children how to construct simple objects. Although it was inspired by the woodwork in his father's Imperial Hotel building in Tokyo, the product's name was selected because of Abraham Lincoln's indelible association with the log cabin, a case of good marketing. This author grew up with a set. Who didn't?

But just as the image of the log cabin conjures up positive sentiment in America, it is also regarded as the uncivilized starting point from which we have worked so hard to advance ourselves as a society. Light-deprived rooms that are too hot or cold and smoky or damp, together with a leaky roof and an utter lack of personal space, are not characteristics that we associate with domestic shelters today, except on camping trips. Because of log architecture's dominance in American national parks, many of us perceive the log cabin as a recreational building type—something designed for those occasions when a tent is unsuitable but we still want to "rough it" in order to commune with nature.

The American Log Cabin and the European Log House

In Central and Eastern Europe and the Scandinavian countries especially, attitudes toward the log house differ markedly. There, for the most part, the log house is the dwelling type of the farmer, widely appreciated and accepted as practical today, just as it has been for hundreds of years. It is a tradition that continues, primarily

In comparing the log buildings of the early United States to those from the same period in Europe, one quickly discovers that very few are extant in America. The William Damm Garrison (1675), originally built in an area of New Hampshire called Dover Neck and used continuously as a residence by members of the Damm family until about 1810, is among the few we have left. Skillfully constructed of square-hewn logs laid on a stone foundation and with a central chimney and eave entry, the one-and-a-half-story Cape Cod–style house is now on the campus of the Woodman Institute in Dover, New Hampshire. Travelers to New England can compare it to Frost Garrison (c. 1738) in Eliot, Maine, also built of square-hewn logs.

because in these nations houses are not repeatedly bought and sold, as has become a common practice in the United States. The house called Gugalun (see pp. 162–67), originally built in 1708, is a good case in point. Nearly three hundred years after it was built, the house remains in the same family. The present owner, like his parents and grandparents before him, inherited the property and did his part to restore it. Since Gugalun is no longer on a working farm, its recent restoration/addition prolongs its relevance in the new role of mountain retreat. Out of respect for tradition, it is highly unlikely that its owner will sell it in order to purchase a condominium nearer the ski lift.

In the old log houses of Central and Eastern Europe and Scandinavia there is also a difference in the quality of craftsmanship, in the durability of construction, and attention to subtle design detail. Even among Modernist architects who live and work in Sweden, Norway, Finland, Austria, Switzerland, Poland, Russia, and Hungary, there is unquestionable respect for the quality of craftsmanship of the old log houses.

A thorough comparison of the construction characteristics of the seventeenth-century American log house with those of an even earlier example from rural Norway, along with the economic circumstances that were likely to have affected each builder, leads one to conclude that the superior craftsmanship of the Norwegian

Throughout the first few decades of the 20th century, America's romance with the Wild West and its typically ramshackle pioneer-style log buildings was partly sparked by the widely popular work of American painter Charles M. Russell (1864–1926), the "Cowboy Artist." In 1903 Russell built this 24-by-30-foot log building as an addition to his house (a traditional frame structure) in Great Falls, Montana. Characterized by a paucity of design consideration and roughly constructed of western red cedar telephone posts, the building served as the artist's studio and is said to have been his favorite space. In the years since Russell's death, the studio, somewhat altered, has become the central focus of Great Falls's C.M. Russell Museum. Each year thousands of individuals form their first impressions of what constitutes a "log cabin" from this building.

example can be attributed not to assets, but to builder pride and know-how. Even in the most remote areas of seventeenth-century Russia, it was not uncommon for log houses to have such details as handcarved window and door surrounds and intricate ridgebeam ornamentation. One would be hard-pressed to find extant, or even in history books, a seventeenth- or even nineteenth-century log building in the United States with that kind of attention to detail.

It is tempting to conclude that the immigrants who came to America and built log houses did so in ways inferior to the customs of their homelands, but some historians would say this is not entirely true. In *Architecture of the United States*, historian Dell Upton suggests that "the majority of log structures were much more carefully crafted than the crude round-log buildings of popular imagination."[3] The inevitable question then is: where in the United States are these carefully crafted early log houses? In Pennsylvania and Virginia[4] there are examples of painstakingly constructed and handsomely designed square-hewn log houses. The Morton Homestead (see p. 12) in Prospect Park, Pennsylvania, formerly the New Sweden colony, is perhaps the most significant among them. Its earliest portion dates to 1698, but it has been added to over the years. Even in its present form, it is a handsome composition, more attractive than many contemporary architect-designed log houses. Still, in terms of craftsmanship this Swedish-immigrant creation fails to measure up to many of the outbuildings preserved at Skansen in Stockholm, Sweden. Why is that?

It begins with the fact that, in the United States, the log house held high in our cultural history and preserved in open-air museums in various parts of the country is more often than not of the sloppily constructed, round-log, and heavily chinked variety. The log house of the United States, unlike those in Switzerland, Austria, Poland, or even the Slovak Republic, began its existence as makeshift housing, a type built on the fly and used only until one's assets grew to the point of making it possible to construct a "proper" frame house with board siding, of the kind found in England. Even immigrants from countries with longstanding log-architecture traditions eventually succumbed to societal pressures and honored the housing traditions of England, where log construction was practically nonexistent.

The American log house's predicament didn't improve to any significant degree until the middle of the nineteenth century, when architects began to work with the idiom. The biggest breakthrough was initiated by amateur architect William West Durant. In 1877, in the first series of buildings that he designed for his Camp Pine Knot on Raquette Lake in New York's Adirondack Mountains, Durant formalized the Adirondack Style. After architect Robert Reamer utilized major aspects in his

At about the same time that Russell completed his log studio in Great Falls, he built another rather unrefined log house on Lake McDonald, in a remote area of Flathead County, Montana (now Glacier National Park). Known as Bull Head Lodge, this was where Russell spent his summers and often entertained many famous friends from the art world. The house still stands today, protected as part of the National Register of Historic Places. In this photograph from 1903, Russell stands next to his wife, Nancy, on the elevated cabin's porch steps with a bull's skull hanging from the unpeeled log course behind them. In 1906 Russell created an enchanting watercolor rendering of this cabin, now in the collection of the Buffalo Bill Historical Center in Cody, Wyoming.

design of Old Faithful Inn at Yellowstone National Park in 1903, the log architecture-based Adirondack Style was adopted for widespread use in national parks across the country. The log-house idiom, soon to be adopted by the Craftsman Movement, had by this point reached a level of refinement that qualified as high art, but in its new capacity as an architecture for recreation it still wasn't taken seriously by the design world's tastemakers.

Altering Perceptions of the Log Cabin

Perceived as a construction method employing old materials and traditional technologies, simple geometries and a predictable aesthetic, the idiom of the log house falls considerably short of the agenda of architectural tastemakers. Even outside the realm of the elite, the log house is too often described by words such as "cozy" or "cute." Unfortunately, the perception will remain thus until the log house is associated with leading figures in the design world. Establishing that association is the mission of this book.

BUILT BY ABRAHAM LINCOLN AND HIS FATHER IN 1831, IN COLES COUNTY, ILLINOIS; TAKEN TO CHICAGO
DURING THE WORLD'S FAIR BY ABRAHAM LINCOLN LOG CABIN ASSOCIATION.

ABOVE The 16th president of the United States, Abraham Lincoln, once lived in this double-pen cabin built by his father about 1831 in Coles County, Illinois. For decades this depressing image, popularized through postcards such as this, symbolized the American log cabin.

RIGHT The idea of the log cabin as recreational architecture evolved from its widespread appropriation—and promotion—by the National Park Service, which was created in August 1916 by President Woodrow Wilson. One of the Park Service's most popular sites has always been the Grand Canyon, where in 1935 its head architect, Mary Colter, designed the round log-constructed Bright Angel Lodge. This is page four of an early ten-page promotional brochure (this particular issue is the 1938 reprint edition) for Grand Canyon's Bright Angel Lodge and Cabins, published in Chicago by the operators of Grand Canyon National Park, the Santa Fe Railroad company. "Rustic log-cabin style" design was a selling point.

THE MAIN LODGE
- - in rustic log-cabin style

Here you may read or write or just "loaf" in the spacious lobby and lounge, with their rustic log beams and huge stone fireplaces . . . or drop into the sunny Coffee Room for a pleasant meal. Information desk and booking office for Grand Canyon motor tours and trail trips are conveniently located in the lobby.

ONLY TWENTY-FIVE FEET
- - from the Canyon's rim

Large sliding doors open from the lounge onto this sunny, stone-flagged terrace, extending to the very brink of the Canyon. And as you gaze down, down, down . . . upon sheer walls and mighty spires of rock bathed in a sea of ever-changing color, you feel the full spell of "this surpassing wonder".

ABOVE Today the William "Buckey" O'Neill Cabin (1889) is the oldest standing building at the Grand Canyon and the most exclusive lodging in the park. Conspicuously situated a mere 30 feet from the edge of the South Rim, next to the reception lobby of the Bright Angel Lodge, the exterior of this thrown-together-on-the-fly pioneer log house has been seen by millions of tourists from all parts of the world. For many individuals, therefore, it represents the idea of the American "log cabin." Unfortunately, O'Neill's double-pen log home receives minimal upkeep, and little attention is paid to its preservation. Instead of showing off what could be a stunning patina of its ancient Utah juniper and pinyon pine logs, the Park Service periodically applies a heavy coat of red paint to the wood, and portions of the logs have been allowed to rot. Worse still is the interior, which features wall-to-wall industrial carpeting and modern fixtures and where no attempt has been made to use period-appropriate furnishings.

Although we will begin with a look at some important prototypes from different parts of the world (including Russia, which we were unable to visit for this book) and briefly consider the important role of the world's fair in prolonging the relevance of the log house in recent history, the heart of this book is a virtual house tour. Here we will explore for the first time examples of log-house architecture designed over the last century or so by a broad range of noteworthy "artist-architects," including Stanislaw Witkiewicz of Poland, Lars Wahlman of Sweden, Adolf Loos of Austria, Alvar Aalto of Finland, Le Corbusier of France, Richard Neutra of California, Peter Zumthor of Switzerland, and Robert A. M. Stern of New York.

The house tour starts at the turn of the twentieth century with the National Romantic movement, the nationalistic fervor that emerged in the 1880s in such nations as Norway, Sweden, Finland, Poland, and Germany and produced the most elaborate examples of single-family log houses in history. It then moves chronologically through most of the major stylistic movements of late-nineteenth- and twentieth-century architecture, including Adirondack Style, Prairie Style, Craftsman, and Modern. We will also examine regional vernacular styles; indeed, this category is represented by some of the most inspired examples of design and craftsmanship in the book. Many of the book's featured houses have never before been published.

SOME PROTOTYPES

TOP In an area along the Delaware River that now constitutes portions of Pennsylvania, Delaware, and New Jersey, immigrants from Sweden in 1638 formed the New Sweden colony in order to establish trade with the Indians. This attractive three-part house made of square-hewn logs, known as the Morton Homestead, is the oldest surviving building from that period. Archaeological studies have determined that the earliest portion dates to about 1698, making it one of the oldest standing log houses in the United States. Writer Sharon Hernes Silverman points out that in terms of construction, the house has its contradictions: "Long grooves that produce tightly fitting log walls are typical of Scandinavian horizontal log technology, as are the lack of mud and clay chinking. . . . On the other hand, the roof framing is Anglo-American in style. The three-room plan approximates the Swedish *parstuga* ["double house" spatial configuration], but it lacks a combination kitchen and entrance."

BOTTOM Whereas in most regions of Norway an old farm typically consisted of a cottage, a loft, and numerous small outbuildings, each with a different function, there evolved in the eastern part of the country a tradition of joining the cottage and loft in order to increase living space and to unite each building's functions for the sake of convenience. Built in 1670 in Tronnes, Osterdal, this is an excellent example of that tradition—what Norwegians call a Barfrostue- or Barfro-cottage farmhouse. Typically, the first floor of the loft portion was treated like an entry hall, equipped with bench seating and a staircase that provided access to the second-floor sleeping area. The rectangular cottage portion would include—in one open space—the living room, dining area, and, next to the fireplace, a space for preparing food. Interior decoration usually consisted of wall paintings or carvings of roses.

OPPOSITE Constructed in 1714, the Church of the Transfiguration of the Savior on Kizhi Island in Lake Onega is the most masterful expression of log architecture in all of Russia. Standing approximately 121 feet high, the building has an octagonal core with four rectangular extensions, each composed of pine logs. The cupolas that sit atop many of its distinctive spade-shaped *bochka* gables are sheathed with as many as 30,000 curved aspen shingles with stepped points. This highly complex structure was made with little more than an axe, an adze, and a drawing knife. The church can still be visited today.

In order that we may better understand the origins of some common forms and details seen in the architect-designed log houses in this book, this chapter offers a visual tour of a few iconic early log buildings, mostly from Northern and Eastern Europe, which were designed and constructed without the benefit of professional designers.

TOP This Norwegian loft building, known as the Tveito Loft, dates to about 1300. It was moved from its original farm site in Hovin, Telemark, to the open-air Norsk Folkmuseum in Oslo, where it may now be studied by the public. Although many lofts from this period were used as storehouses for food and clothing, the arrangement of this particular building suggests that it was used primarily for living. It has an open room with benches on the first level, and upstairs, surrounded by the cantilevered gallery, is a space that holds two small beds. As a form, the loft is of enormous importance, and its defining attributes appear in a number of the houses featured in this book. It is essential to understand that the horizontal log core of the first floor in fact extends up through the stave-constructed second floor to help support the roof, which also has a ridgebeam. The core therefore defines the space of the second-floor gallery. Access to the second floor is provided by a stair, which is concealed behind the V-shaped beam assembly positioned to the right of the first-floor door. Once up those stairs and into the portion of the gallery behind the façade's vertically hung planks and small arcades is a door similar to that on the first floor, complete with elaborate carvings of acanthus, lions, and a bear's head.

BOTTOM The Halvorsgard Lofthouse, an example of the common integration of the loft building and cottage, was built about 1750 in Hol, Hallingdal, Norway, where the loft-house type is said to have originated. The vertically hung panels of the second-floor gallery (which is present on two sides of the building) feature decorative carvings and perforations. Below the gallery, on the near side, is the entrance. Typically, the first floor consists of a living room with benches, a corner bed, and a fireplace, and the galleried second floor, cantilevered over corbelled logs, was used either for sleeping or for entertaining guests. Before the 17th century, this building would not have had a fireplace, and it was not until the 18th century that such buildings were given windows. Halvorsgard Lofthouse, although compact, is nicely proportioned and has impeccable corner joinery.

TOP The Oshevnev House (1876) was originally built in the Russian village of Oshevnevo for the family of a well-to-do peasant named Nestor Grigorievich Oshevnev and is now an open-air museum on the island of Kizhi. It is a prime example of a typical Russian *koshel* house, in which the living space and the working space (a cattle shed and hayloft) are placed under a single asymmetrical gable roof. To understand the spatial arrangement of the house as depicted in this photograph, one should note that the ridgebeam is placed directly in the center of the living space portion, the *izba*. The protruding log ends to the left of the hayloft ramp mark the boundary between the living and working spaces. The ornamentation, which is characteristic of the period, consists of baroque window decoration, balconies with turned posts, infill panels carved in floral motifs, elaborately carved extended bargeboards, and a carved ridgebeam head.

BOTTOM In the village of Chocholow, a short drive east of the town of Zakopane in Poland, there are groups of beautifully preserved 19th-century Polish highlander cottages—the very houses that provided much of the source material for architect Stanislaw Witkiewicz's Zakopane Style.

THE LOG HOUSE
AND THE
WORLD'S FAIRS

Beginning in the latter half of the nineteenth century, the log house's relevance as a building type was continually reinforced on an international level through its presence at several of the world's fairs that took place in a number of European and American cities. Although the log house was predominantly a theme utilized by the Scandinavians, it was also harnessed by other nations and states to represent their respective heritages. In nearly every instance, the buildings were excellent, finely handcrafted examples.

The Paris Exposition Universelle of 1867 in France included Sweden's replica of a fifteenth-century farmhouse, the Ornässtuga, which was a loft building with a log-constructed ground floor and a shingled frame structure above it. Norway was represented at the fair by a replica of an iconic Norwegian loft building, which combined stave and horizontal log construction.

There were also a number of log houses at the 1876 Philadelphia Centennial Exposition in America. Sweden installed the Swedish Schoolhouse Building, a sophisticated structure of horizontal log construction designed by the firm of Isaeus & Jacobsson. Standing a story-and-a-half tall and encompassing about 3,000 square feet, the building featured two fireplaces with tall decorative chimney stacks, along with classically inspired arched windows set between protruding corbelled logs that supported the deeply overhanging eaves. Also on display at the Philadelphia fair was a log building submitted by the state of Mississippi. True to the log-building traditions of America's pioneers, the construction consisted of round logs laid horizontally with a cross-gabled roof over one and a half stories. The most prominent feature may have been its swamp moss, which had been liberally hung from its eaves to provide the kind of ornament Mother Nature would have supplied in rural Mississippi. The house was also appointed with balustrades made of twisted bark-covered branches—an overtly rustic structure-as-ornament design element that had been prescribed by Andrew Jackson Downing in his book *The Architecture of Country Houses* (1850).

The World's Columbian Exposition of 1893, held on 633 acres of downtown Chicago's Jackson Park, attracted more than twenty-seven million visitors from around the world. The fair's appeal was largely architectural, with more than two hundred buildings representing thirty-eight states and seventy-nine foreign countries. Whereas its main structures conformed to the fair planners' "White City Style" (what we now refer to as Beaux-Arts Classicism), those submitted by the states and foreign nations were supposed to showcase their respective architectural traditions. A number of the buildings featured log craftsmanship and construction. The critically acclaimed Idaho State Building by architect Kirtland Cutter (1860–1939) of Cutter and Poetz Architects in Spokane, Washington, was a three-story house made of Idaho cedar logs laid horizontally. Shaped in a loose adaptation of the popular

OPPOSITE, TOP For the Paris Exposition Universelle of 1867, Sweden delivered the Ornässtuga, a replica of a 15th-century farmhouse.

BOTTOM Norway's entry was this richly detailed loft building.

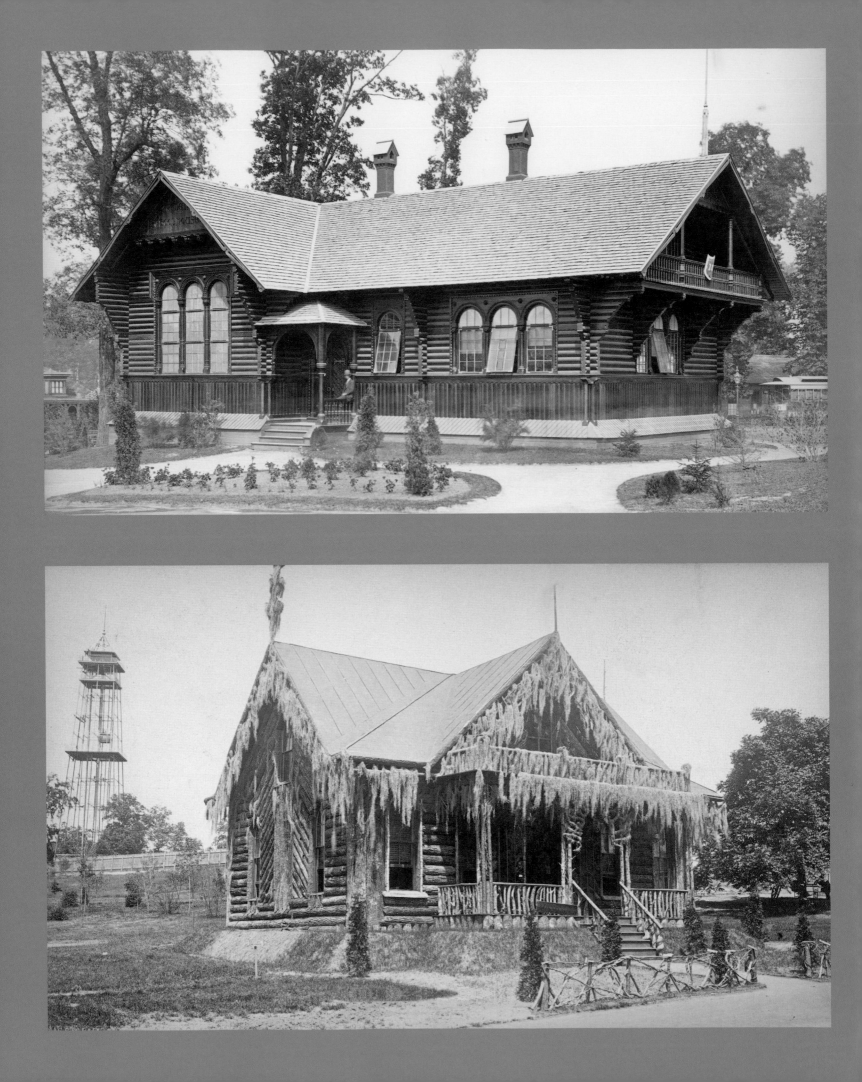

OPPOSITE, TOP At the 1876 Philadelphia Centennial Exposition, Sweden again produced a log building, the Swedish Schoolhouse, which was composed of Baltic fir and cost about $7,000. After the fair, the building was moved to Central Park in New York City, where it eventually became the Marionette Theater. It was completely restored in 1997.

BOTTOM The other prominent log house at the 1876 Philadelphia Centennial Exposition was the Mississippi State Building, built by the Mississippi Valley Industrial Company of McComb City. Its construction, the views of which were partially obscured by the Spanish moss attached to the house for effect, was said to have utilized 68 varieties of native-Mississippi timber grown in Pike and Lincoln Counties.

BELOW On view at the Chicago World's Fair of 1893 was this substantial log house, the Idaho State Building, designed by architect Kirtland Cutter. At the turn of the century, Cutter was one of the most skilled designers of large-scale log buildings. He would go on to design the similarly impressive Kootenai Lodge (c. 1906) in Big Fork, Montana, and Lake McDonald Lodge (1913) in Glacier National Park.

Swiss Chalet Style, the Idaho building, like the Swedish Schoolhouse Building of 1876, featured deeply overhanging eaves that rested on protruding corbelled logs. Cutter gave it one of the grandest entry gestures of all the fair's state buildings by placing the front doorway in the massive base of the gable-end rough-stone chimneystack. The effect created a dramatic cavernlike entrance that led to the interior's equally rustic exposed-log walls and lava-rock floors. As historian Henry C. Matthews pointed out, "The Idaho Building stood for only a few months yet its significance was very real. . . . Cutter had glorified natural materials and rustic construction in a structure of almost heroic scale."[1] Three years after the fair, Matthews noted, one of its visitors, Arthur Heneage Lloyd of England, commissioned Cutter to create virtually the same house for a densely forested plot that he owned in Hampshire.[2]

Another building at the 1893 fair that involved highly refined log construction was the Norwegian Building, designed by Waldemar Hansteen, a noted Norwegian church architect. This re-creation of a small Norwegian stave church was symmetrically shaped with a steeply pitched gabled roof; its horizontal and vertical logs were hewn square in keeping with stave-church tradition. This particular building remains intact today as a museum house called Little Norway, located in Blue Mounds, Wisconsin, and it is listed on the National Register of Historic Places.

The Paris Exposition Universelle of 1900 was devoted primarily to examples of the emerging Art Nouveau Style, but impressive log buildings were also displayed, the most significant being those of the Swiss Village. This 69,000-square-foot section of the fair featured multiple log buildings constructed in the Swiss Chalet Style. The highly accurate representations took Switzerland's team of three hundred builders three years to complete.

At the Pan Pacific Exposition of 1915–16 in San Francisco, rustic log construction made another appearance. Architect Bernard Maybeck (1862–1957) created the House of Hoo-Hoo for the Pacific Lumbermen's Association. According to a guidebook to the exposition published that year, it was an impressive entry. "There is little used but rough-barked tree trunks, but what delicate harmony of arrangement! This lumbermen's lodge is one building outside the Exposition palaces that should not be missed, even though almost hidden away against the south wall. It is worth pondering over. No one may want to build a house like it, but it proclaims how beauty can be attained with simple materials and just proportions."[3]

More recently, at Chicago's Century of Progress Exposition in 1933–34, architect Murray D. Hetherington created the Cypress Log Cabin for the Southern Cypress Manufacturers' Association. One of the few houses constructed for the fair using traditional materials, the cabin served as a showcase for cypress artifacts. It still stands today, under the administration of the National Park Service, and can be visited by the public at the Indian Dunes National Lakeshore in Beverly Shores, Indiana.[4]

The high-art log house's appearance between 1867 and 1934 on these international stages would have inevitably driven it to the attention of architects and potential homeowners. Consequently, the fairs are responsible to a significant extent for its continued relevance today.

TOP Norwegian architect Waldemar Hansteen's stave church represented Norway at the 1893 Chicago World's Fair.

BOTTOM A postcard from the Paris Exposition Universelle of 1900 illustrates the many expertly crafted Swiss chalet-style log buildings that made up Switzerland's Swiss Village at the fair.

TOP Architect Bernard Maybeck's House of Hoo-Hoo at the Pan Pacific Exposition of 1915–16 in San Francisco. Compare its massive tree-trunk columns to those in architect Roland Terry's own house built some five decades later (see page 130).

BOTTOM The front elevation of Cypress Log Cabin, the house designed by architect Murray D. Hetherington for Chicago's Century of Progress Exhibition, 1933–34

The art of placing one log on top of the other and thus forming a perpendicular, solid and air-tight wall, actually is but a humble task, the practical expression of a jointer's handicraft, though craving care and perspicacity in its execution. It is a form of architecture the origin of which can be traced back to the oldest civilization of the Mediterranean basin, to royal castles and humble dwelling houses of Homer's world and to temple-buildings of the early Hellenes.

Georg Eliassen, *Norwegian Architecture throughout the Ages*

The Tour

Frögnerseteren

LOCATION
Oslo, Norway

YEAR BUILT
1890

ARCHITECT
Holm Hansen Munthe

STYLE
Dragon

From Oslo center, the Holmenkollveien road swerves dramatically northward into a mountainous suburban area that looks out over the city and the adjacent bay—the shimmering Oslofjorden. Once you get above the Holmenkollen National Ski Jump Arena, site of the 1952 Winter Olympics, and into the area called Tryvann Hill, Frögnerseteren and its commanding location in the vast Oslo-Marka forest some 1,427 feet above the fjord, come into view. In a nation whose log-construction traditions are representative of the highest order of handcraftsmanship, demonstrated in extant examples that date as far back as the 1300s, it is significant that Frögnerseteren is one of Norway's greatest log houses.

The modern beginnings of Frögnerseteren's site can be traced to 1865, the year that Thomas Heftye, a local banker and cofounder of the Norwegian Association of Tourism, assumed its ownership as part of a larger land acquisition. He subsequently built a little turf-roofed cabin, which has been restored and still receives visitors just below the parking area in front of Frögnerseteren. Then, as now, the area was popular as a scenic stopping point for downhill and cross-country skiers. After Heftye's death in 1886, his widow oversaw the vast property and its holdings until 1889, when the city of Christiania[1] acquired from her a 1,926-acre section of the property called Frögnerseteren Wood, with the intention of developing its naturally exceptional recreational terrain. Here the city's leaders decided to build an array of facilities and a resort complex consisting of hotel buildings and restaurants, all of which would embody Norway's growing national optimism.

By 1889 the forty-one-year-old Norwegian architect Holm Hansen Munthe (1848–1898), who had been working locally in Christiania since forming his own firm there in 1878, was well on his way toward devising what would be recognized as Norway's first national building style, an appropriately picturesque mode that honored the "Norsemen's" rich heritage of sublime wood architecture.[2]

At this point in time, for the design of its new freestanding houses, Norwegian architects (most of whom customarily received at least part of their training and initial professional practice in Germany) and amateur designer/builders alike had made what Germans call the "Swiss Style" their primary reference source, adapting it to the vernacular of any given site. Historian Barbara Miller Lane describes the origins of this style: "In Germany the early nineteenth-century tradition of building rustic dwellings on the great princely estates, exemplified by the log mansion Nikolskoye in Berlin of 1827 and the so-called Russian Colony in Potsdam of 1826, soon developed into a widespread preference among the well-to-do for a 'Swiss style' in housing: a wooden architecture with horizontal wood siding, high-peaked roofs, and some kind of Swiss, Bavarian, or Tyrolean accents of carved wood or half-timbering. The Swiss style was relatively short-lived in Germany, but in the Scandinavian countries it led to a series of important revivals: the 'Gothic,' or 'Old Norse,' revival in Sweden and the 'dragon style' in Norway."[3]

Norwegian architect Holm Hansen Munthe's Dragon Style designs often directly reference the iconic form and certain details of the medieval Norwegian loft building. This close-up view of the loft wing of Frögnerseteren's front elevation brings into focus a row of decoratively perforated panels, which sheathe the lower portion of the overhanging second floor, as well as its nearly seven-foot-high stone foundation. Both levels serve as dining rooms.

Not to be confused with the Swiss Chalet Style, the Swiss Style will be familiar to American readers who are acquainted with the mode of architecture known in the United States as the Stick Style, which proliferated in this country from about 1840 to the late 1870s and was identified by American historian Vincent Scully.[4] Christian Norberg-Schulz, an expert in Norwegian architecture, suggests that the Swiss Style was introduced in Christiania/Oslo as early as 1839, the year the palace architect H. D. F. Linstow began work on his own house there after studying wooden architecture in Germany. By 1850 the style had found widespread popularity in Norway, as well as in Sweden and Finland.[5] In Norway, however, as elsewhere on the European continent by the late 1880s, there was a romantic yearning for an architecture that spoke of the country's growing national spirit and its unique and endearing architectural traditions (never mind the fact that at this time Norway was still joined with Sweden under a common king). It was inevitable that interest in the Swiss Style—particularly among academics, artists, and architects—soon began to move toward the architecture and design details of the stave churches of Norway's countryside (see page 20).[6]

By now Munthe had designed a number of buildings in the Swiss Style, and he appropriated some of its characteristics—in particular the larger window sizes, ornate porches, and decorative trusses—to create his first Dragon Style work, a bath house (1880) in the city of Larvik. He borrowed the arched window shapes and prominent roof cresting of the stave church, along with other details, both structural and ornamental. More significantly, however, he added certain iconic features unique to the medieval Norwegian loft building (also known as the storehouse): a structural core of notched-log construction; a cantilevered (galleried loft) second floor that typically rested on corbelled logs; decoratively perforated infill panels set vertically between massive turned second-floor corner posts; and a front-facing low-pitched gabled roof with intricately carved wide bargeboards and deeply overhanging eaves. The resulting form was given the name "Dragon Style" because of its other distinguishing architectural feature—the stave church's gable-crowning dragon's heads. A Viking motif, this peculiar wooden ornament was originally conceived and utilized by church leaders during the Middle Ages in order to warn off evil.

"Munthe's bathing house at Larvik," says Norberg-Schulz of this image, "his first work in this [dragon] style, was immediately recognized as a significant contribution to the development of a Norwegian national identity in the arts."[7] Thus, by 1889, Munthe had positioned himself as the city's most obvious choice as architect of the ambitious design program of the resort buildings at Tryvann Hill.

Later that same year, a large portion of the sloping site's Norway-spruce forest was cleared and construction begun on the first building Munthe designed for the site, the log-constructed Holmenkollen Tourist Hotel (1889–90). It was destroyed by fire shortly thereafter but was rebuilt in 1895–96.

Frögnerseteren, which was completed in 1890, very quickly became a national sensation, providing an idiom for building with logs that would be adopted by professional and layman designers and builders for homes, hotels, hunting lodges, and restaurants throughout Norway and beyond during the decade that followed.[8] The

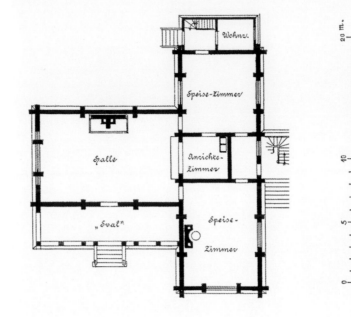

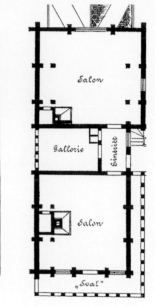

ABOVE, TOP By the time Frögnerseteren was under construction, the Norwegian log-joinery technique of full-scribe joinery, as seen in this saddle-notched corner, had been in use for more than 600 years. The technique involves scribing, or cutting, the bottom of each stacking log so that its surface matches the top surface of the log below it; this results in a locking fit that requires little or no insulation. The corners are held together not only by the saddle notch, but also by an internal joint that is sized to accommodate post-construction shrinkage. It locks into place under the wall's own weight. This was all accomplished with a tool kit that consisted of little more than handsaws and a handforged axe, a chisel, a curved draw knife, and what's called a scratch scriber. It is still possible to have a log home built in Norway using this method.

ABOVE, BOTTOM Logs must be periodically replaced, a normal form of maintenance in a log home. This section, however, dates to Frögnerseteren's original 1890 construction, its integrity still sound. Between each log are small fibers for insulation, primarily consisting of horse and other animal hair.

ABOVE, RIGHT The original T-shaped first-floor plan (left). The additional wing was added off the hall, at the bottom of the T. The second-floor plan (right), designated for dining, remains much the same as originally depicted here.

most famous of these is probably the sprawling Dalen Hotel (1894) in Telemark, Norway, a Dragon Style design by architect Haldor Larsen Børve (1857–1933), which received a complete restoration during the 1990s.

Munthe would continue to work in the Dragon Style. Immediately after Frögnerseteren, in 1891, he completed the Pavilion Hans Haugens in Oslo and, in the village of Rominten, Germany (then East Prussia), he designed for Emperor Wilhelm II a massive stave church and an equally spectacular Dragon Style hunting lodge. His Dragon Style sport pavilion near Frögnerseteren was completed in 1896, and in 1897 he was appointed to the distinguished position of city architect for Christiania. He died a year later.

In 1913, four years after the end of Norway's union with Sweden, because the number of visitors to Frögnerseteren had reached an overwhelming level, the building received a new wing, which projected off the front and rear elevations, to the left of the bay that contains the front entrance. The building's owner, along with highly skilled local builders and craftspeople, honored the importance of what Munthe had originally created by seeing to it that the addition was seamlessly integrated with the existing structure. Today, some 115 years after its origination, Frögnerseteren appears much as it did nearly a century ago when it was enlarged; little else has changed except for periodic restoration work to the logs, roof, and chimneys and the necessary modernization of the building's mechanical appliances.

RIGHT From this table in the first floor's front dining room, situated just to the right of the front entryway, one is afforded stunning views of the city of Oslo and the Oslofjorden below.

BELOW, LEFT This is the great hall, the room one encounters upon entering the building through the front door. This part of the building, including the fireplace, is all original. In the background is a staircase that leads to the second-floor dining rooms.

BELOW, RIGHT As the plan illustrates, the second floor's front dining room also has a fireplace. Notice the boards of the ceiling, each painted in a variety of floral and animal motifs. The smaller room in the background, the cantilevered portion of the loft wing, has the best views of all.

Ravine Lodge

LOCATION
Highland Park, Illinois

YEAR BUILT
1893

ARCHITECT
William W. Boyington

STYLE
Adirondack

This is the view of Ravine Lodge from the street, what was originally the back of the house. Because of its many additions and modifications, this is a difficult house to read, but it is in fact a simple layout. The projecting wing at the far right end was added at some point after the original construction. It now contains the kitchen and above it a guest bedroom. The middle portion of the house has the breakfast room with bedrooms above, and the far left section contains, from bottom to top, a three-car garage, a great room, and additional bedrooms.

OPPOSITE, TOP The side of the house that was the original front elevation looks out onto 17-acre Millard Park and the shore of Ravine Beach. In order to understand the degree to which the house has been modified, compare this view to that of the period photograph of the same elevation on the next page. The door at the top of the wrap-around cedar deck stair opens to the living room, which makes it easy for summertime entertaining to spill into the outdoors.

BOTTOM The bark on the logs has been periodically replaced throughout the life of the house. Unfortunately, the occasional need to increase the insulating chinking between each log has resulted in a less-than-tidy appearance of the log course. For the most part, a mixture of lime mortar and sand was used, as shown here. In recent years, the log-building industry has developed a latex substance made especially for chinking log houses.

In 1892 Sylvester M. Millard of the prestigious Chicago law firm of Millard & Hale hired one of America's most distinguished architects, William W. Boyington, to design a country home for his newly purchased twenty-six-acre site near Lake Michigan's Ravine Beach, some two dozen miles north of downtown Chicago. The house Boyington ultimately gave him differed considerably from the mostly Victorian-era Italianate and Gothic Revival–style vacation homes in this growing Chicago suburb. It was sited next to a stream on a large, densely forested lot, where it did not compete with its lush natural surroundings but seemed to grow out of them.

Befitting its site, the house would be constructed of logs, and a certain rustic elegance would distinguish its design. It was a look that is present to some degree in any number of rural areas of the United States where expert woodcrafters have worked in log construction, but it was formalized in 1877 in the hands of William West Durant, a developer and amateur architect from the Adirondack Mountain region in New York State. In Durant's first multi-building retreat, called Camp Pine Knot, the first of the so-called Adirondack Great Camps,[1] the practice of using logs structurally and twisted branches, roots, and strips of bark for ornament had been elevated to a level that some were then calling fine art.[2] By the time Boyington began to shape the design of Millard's house on the outskirts of Chicago, the Pine Knot look, known as the Adirondack Style, had evolved into a legitimate design idiom, widely appropriated in the region of its origin and quickly gaining popularity across the United States. Within a decade after the Millard House was completed, the Adirondack Style had spread as far west as Montana, where it was utilized by architect Robert Reamer in his design of the Old Faithful Inn (1903) at Yellowstone National Park. Eventually it would characterize thousands of buildings created by the National Parks Service for its parks across the country.

Millard had worked with Boyington before the construction of the house they called Ravine Lodge, as had many of Chicago's leading businessmen.[3] Born in Southwick, Massachusetts, Boyington (1818–1898) moved to Chicago in the fall of 1853 and promptly founded one of the city's first architectural firms, W. W. Boyington & Co., Chicago, Architects. At the time, Chicago had no more than a few dozen architects to its credit, Edward Burling, Otto H. Matz, and John M. Van Osdel among them. Boyington had not gone to school to study architecture, however, but had learned through hands-on experience working in the Boston area for his father, who was reportedly a self-made master builder known for handling certain design duties for his projects.[4] Within a decade of his arrival in Chicago, Boyington had established himself as one of the city's leading architects, and he eventually completed more than two hundred works in the Chicago area—churches, houses, department stores, office buildings, hotels, theaters, train depots, and other types of structures.[5]

In 1869, when the American Institute of Architects (AIA) Chicago Chapter was founded, its members elected Boyington to be its first president, giving him unrivaled clout among Chicago's tightly knit group of design professionals. (He would go on to serve several consecutive terms for the AIA in this position.) That same year he also served as a director of the Chicago Building and Loan Association, a position that afforded him relationships with some of the biggest spenders in the Midwest. Boyington's legacy was forever solidified, however, after his 154-foot-high Gothic-style Chicago Water Works Tower, built in 1869 on Pine Street (now Michigan Avenue), emerged as one of the few monumental buildings in the city to survive its Great Fire of 1871. His Illinois State Building for the 1893 World's Columbian Exposition in Chicago made its debut the same year Boyington completed the Millards' country home.

A year earlier he had designed the Millards' apartment in downtown Chicago,[6] but soon after the log house was completed, the apartment lost its designation as their primary address. In 1896, after the house had been winterized, the Millards moved into it for good,[7] and for the next century at least one member of the Millard family would reside there. Along the way, inevitably, many changes were made to the original design.

The illustrations of Ravine Lodge that were first published in the November 1892 issue of the *Inland Architect and News Record* are all that survive showing the house's original appearance. The photographs reveal that a gable originally projected off the front elevation, complete with a balcony below the roof valley formed by the intersecting gables. In keeping with the Adirondack Style, the balcony's balustrade was elaborately constructed of twisted branches and roots.

BELOW, LEFT The master bedroom is 24 feet wide by 21 feet deep and has 15-foot vaulted ceilings. Steel tension rods reach across the width of the room to support the construction. In the back corner is the door that leads to a modernized master bathroom.
BELOW, RIGHT In the foreground are large walk-in closets, which separate the master bedroom from its bathroom, where a limestone steam shower and a cast-iron whirlpool tub await.

OPPOSITE The great room is 42 feet wide by 25 feet deep and has the original 11-inch-wide oak-plank floors. The hewn Illinois elm log walls of this room are original, as are the ceiling beams. Both have been bleached and oiled.

At a subsequent though still early date (the Highland Park Building Department's records go back only as far as 1920), the balcony, which would have allowed clear views of the beach from the house, was given a shed roof that made the outdoor room a more practical component of a house being used year-round. Eventually, however, the covered balcony was demolished, along with the entire projecting gable, and the width of the front elevation was broadened by approximately thirty feet. This made possible the addition of the second fireplace in the great room, the stairway behind it, and what are now the dining room on the first floor and, above it, the master bedroom with cathedral ceilings nearly fifteen feet high. Other alterations include the addition of a dormered window above the master bedroom to allow in more natural light. Typical of full log construction, however, each of these structural changes is revealed in the unusual rearrangement of the logs (their protruding ends in particular).

In 1982 Ravine Lodge, one of the earliest extant examples of an Adirondack style single-family residence designed by a major architect and the only log house designed by Boyington, was added to the National Register of Historic Places. One of Sylvester Millard's grandchildren finally sold the house outside the family in 1996; it has changed ownership three times since then, selling most recently for $2 million.

RIGHT A close-up view of the house's century-old rough-hewn Illinois elm

BELOW When this room was added to the house, care was taken to match the floorboards to those of the living room. However, when the log walls were added (as the wall in the background reveals), the builder broke with tradition and opted to leave the surfaces of the logs round and to introduce Sheetrock, utilized here on the ceiling.

OPPOSITE The kitchen has become the primary gathering place in the American home, and even the owners of historically important properties are compelled to update their kitchens with the latest appliances and fixtures. Often in log houses, the rustic theme ends at the entrance to the kitchen. This is a 21st-century room in a late-19th-century house.

Dom Pod Jedlami

LOCATION
Zakopane, Poland

YEAR BUILT
1897

ARCHITECT
Stanislaw Witkiewicz

BUILDER
Jan Obrochta Bartusiow

STYLE
Zakopane

The rear elevation of Dom Pod Jedlami, a beautifully restored masterpiece of the Zakopane Style. Although the half gables, superlative log work, and much of the stick work come from local building traditions, the form of the house has strong Queen Anne–style characteristics, recalling aspects of prototypical examples such as Leyes Wood (1868) in Surrey by England's Richard Norman Shaw and H. H. Richardson's William Watts Sherman House (1874) in Newport, Rhode Island.

Stanislaw Witkiewicz was banished from his native Poland to Siberia in 1864 at the age of twelve for helping his parents and other Polish insurgents obtain food, gunpowder, and various other supplies in the 1863 uprising against Russia, but this is only one of several distinctions that set him apart from his peers. Witkiewicz went on to become an award-winning painter, poet, journalist, art critic, novelist, theoretician, educator, and furniture designer, and today he is considered a Polish national hero for his wide-ranging contributions to the arts. Although his extraordinary legacy can now be mined to a degree in the holdings of libraries and art museums in certain parts of the world, it exists in its purest, most engaging form at the foot of the soaring Tatra Mountains, in the village of Zakopane.

Dom Pod Jedlami, Polish for "the House under the Firs," is the fifth house designed by Witkiewicz, and it is regarded as the flagship of the Zakopane Style. It was commissioned by Jan Gwalbert Pawlikowski, a wealthy and highly educated man whose family had vast land holdings across Poland.[1] Originally from Medyka, Poland, the Pawlikowskis were strong supporters of Witkiewicz's artistic endeavors and approached him about designing a house for them after seeing his Villa Koliba (1892; now open to the public as a museum), Villa Pepita (1893), Villa Oksza (1895), and Villa Zofiowka (1895)—each built not far from the Pawlikowski site and designed in the then-evolving Zakopane idiom.

The Zakopane Style is Witkiewicz's response to the national romanticism that swept across Poland in the final decade of the nineteenth century. In certain aspects of both design and construction, it references such international sources as Philip Webb's Red House (1859) and Henry Hobson Richardson's William Watts Sherman House (1874), particularly the latter. The style also derives from the prototypical eighteenth- and nineteenth-century highlander cottages of the Podhale region, including a few early examples that can still be found in central Zakopane and the nearby village of Chochołów (see page 15).

The highlander cottage's characteristic shingle-covered roof with multiple half gables,[2] along with its decorative Podhale-inspired wall-surface stickwork in the gable ends, is apparent in all examples of Witkiewicz's architecture. He also uses its highlander-motif ornamentation (carved by hand or burned in), a feature that was customarily applied around the framing of windows and doors and on balconies, as well as on its wide eaves, which force the frequent snow, snowmelt, and rain to fall away from the house's foundation. Whereas the early Polish highlander houses were usually placed directly on the ground or on low stone piers, Witkiewicz at Dom Pod Jedlami introduced a monumental Neo-Romanesque foundation of stone with round-arched fenestration, much like that which had become commonplace in the work of Richardson a decade earlier.

Most significantly, Witkiewicz uses the highlander cottage's core construction of massive rough-sawn squared logs (usually spruce)—each square-notched, uniquely tongued and grooved at the corners for a locking fit when stacked, and chinked with peculiar, minuscule, wool-like wood shavings.

"The idea for the creation of a national style on the basis of the vernacular construction of Podhale," explains historian Zbigniew Mozdzierz of the Tatra Museum, "may have emerged under the influence of the Russian style based on related intellectual foundations, with which Stanislaw Witkiewicz might have come into contact during his studies at the St. Petersburg Academy of Fine Arts between 1868 and 1871."[3] The seeds for the idea could also have been planted in Witkiewicz's mind in the mid-1870s, however, after he left his fine-art studies at the Royal Academy of Fine Arts in Munich, and again in the mid- to late 1880s. During these two periods of his life, he was in Warsaw, where he was very much part of the city's burgeoning intellectual scene, working first as a painter and later as an art critic.

Throughout the 1880s, as we have seen in the case of Norway, there existed in several nations of Northern, Eastern, and Central Europe a romanticism that eventually led to various attempts to create national styles of architecture. Historian Jan Zachwatowicz suggests that Poland's quest for a national style had its beginnings in Krakow, drawing inspiration from the culture of Zakopane and the surrounding area: "At the end of the nineteenth century, within the preponderant trend of eclecticism, attempts at a new look at architectural form became increasingly apparent. In Krakow, a movement gained momentum in search for forms of a 'native' Polish architecture, based on folk art, especially that of the Podhale mountain region."[4]

For Witkiewicz the desire to create a style that would honor his nation's past while guiding it in the future was certainly cemented after his first visit to Zakopane,

in 1886.[5] He was immediately taken with the culture of the Tatras and the folk-architecture traditions of the Podhale region, and he wrote a series of celebratory literary and journalistic works that began to see publication in Warsaw later that year. Among them is *Tatry w śniegu* (The Tatra Mountains in the Snow, 1886), in which Witkiewicz comments specifically on the residential architecture of the place: "The cottage of the *górale* [local Tatra Mountain people] is a superior type of architecture, in which the decoration of the utilitarian is a manifestation of definite aesthetic needs."[6]

In 1890, with his health again in decline (a decade earlier he had suffered through bouts of tuberculosis), Witkiewicz moved his permanent residence to Zakopane, where four years earlier the village had been given official status as a health resort because of its superior air quality. When Witkiewicz eventually recovered, he began mapping out his concepts for the Zakopane Style.

From the very beginning, he hired only local master carpenters and craftspeople to execute his designs, and he was known to supervise the highlanders in nearly every detail.[7] Dom Pod Jedlami was no exception. When it came to the house's interiors, the flooring, walls, and ceiling of which are constructed of unfinished planks of pine or fir, Witkiewicz was completely involved and brought an artist's eye to each detail.[8] He designed one of the house's highly ornate tile-and-stone heating stoves, which are inspired by those commonly found in the early highlander cottages, as well as the drawing room's elaborate fireplace and a number of wood furnishings, including a cupboard, shelving unit, bench, bed, armchairs, and table and chairs. The rest of the house's furnishings were designed and built by other local master craftsmen.[9]

Each piece of furniture was given prominent hand-carved ornamentation in common highlander motifs, such as the rosette and heart and bell shapes. Ornamentation was also applied to the doors and door frames, exposed ceiling beams, and the mantelpiece, among other surfaces—in some instances carved and then painted in a variety of highlander folk art–inspired vegetal motifs. Just as Witkiewicz had prescribed, the house's interiors are a symphony of beautifully ornamented blond wood, creating a *Gesamtkunstwerk* (total art work), a concept that had been introduced in 1849 by German composer Richard Wagner and was later adopted by members of England's Arts and Crafts Movement.

In the summer of 1897, the Pawlikowskis stayed at Dom Pod Jedlami for the first time, and in 1931 the Polish government formally recognized the house as a national monument (a protective status it holds to this day). The house survived World War II, having been spared by the Nazis thanks to the absence of electricity in the building.[10] Since the war, Dom Pod Jedlami has received a number of sensitively applied restorations in order to maintain the integrity of its original appearance. Throughout its long history, celebrated painters, writers, actors, filmmakers, government officials, and other high-profile guests from various parts of the world have visited the house and admired it.[11] Before he became Pope John Paul II, Cardinal Karol Wojtyla came to see Dom Pod Jedlami and gave it his blessing before he went on to Rome.

ABOVE Master carpenters of the Tatra Mountains have traditionally built their homes of square-hewn logs that lock into place with dowel rods and with special square-notch joinery, as at Dom Pod Jedlami. The insulation between each log consists of tiny wood shavings that have a ropelike consistency.

OPPOSITE The jigsaw-cut ornamentation on the entry passage. The heart with turk's-cap lily is an example of Witkiewicz's prominent use of Art Nouveau motifs in the house.

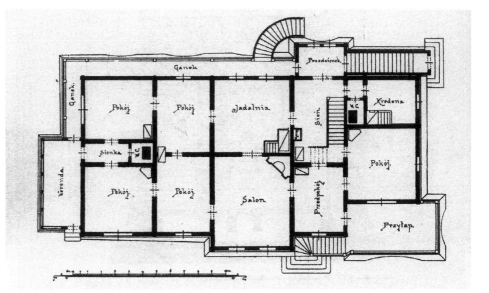

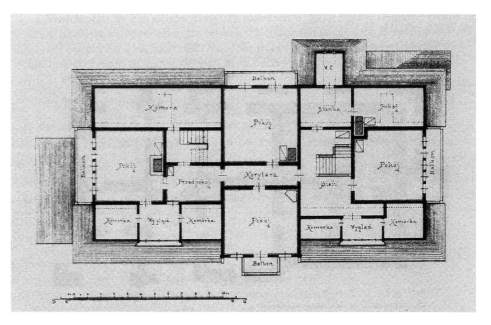

LEFT, TOP As in the rest of the house, the dining room features an abundance of finely detailed woodcarvings. Note the rosettes on the ceiling beams and the turk's-cap lilies on the door at left, which leads to the drawing room. The cupboard dates to 1898 and, like the Witkiewicz–designed table and chairs, was built specifically for the house.

LEFT, BOTTOM The drawing room's tile fireplace, all original, has painted ornamentation of turk's-cap lilies, rosettes, and heart shapes, along with a crouching bear holding a clock. According to Witkiewicz expert Zbigniew Mozdzierz, this particular fireplace, unlike the other, simpler ones in the house, does not follow local design tradition but was created specifically for Dom Pod Jedlami.

RIGHT, TOP The first-floor plan, as redrawn by Eugeniusz Wesolowski in 1910. Although it does not specify the exact function of every room (*pokoj* means "room"), some can be identified. For example, *jadalnia* is the dining room, which is shown in the photograph at the left. Labeled *salon* is the drawing room, where the fireplace shown on

this page is situated. Unlike other houses of this period, Jedlami's first-floor rooms are not organized around a great hall and reflect a plan that is less than progressive for its time. The kitchen and other service functions are in the cellar.

RIGHT, BOTTOM Because Jedlami was used as a retreat for a large family and their guests, the second floor was designed with many bedrooms.

OPPOSITE Another view of the drawing room, the area just to the right of the tile fireplace. The furnishings shown here were made for the house in late 1902 and early 1903 by local highlander Wojciech Brzega.

Hvitträsk

LOCATION
Kirkkonummi, Finland

YEAR BUILT
1903

ARCHITECTS
Herman Gesellius, Armas Lindgren,
and Eliel Saarinen

BUILDER
Hjalmar Lindroos

STYLE
Finnish National Romantic

Here at the edge of Lake Vitträsk, about fifteen miles southwest of Helsinki in the town of Kirkkonummi, the towering Finnish pines and white birch that envelop Hvitträsk, a compound of log-and-granite houses, creak and moan as they accommodate the icy gusts of wind rolling off the frozen lake. This is the scenery that ultimately inspired three young architects, Herman Gesellius, Armas Lindgren, and Eliel Saarinen, to choose this remote place for their shared house/ studio in 1901.

In 1895, while they were students in the architecture program at Helsinki's Polytechnic Institute, Saarinen (1873–1950), best known as designer of the master plan of the Cranbrook School (1928) in Bloomfield Hills, Michigan; Lindgren (1874–1929); and Gesellius (1874–1916) formed the friendships that would eventually lead them to Lake Vitträsk. It was at the Institute that each of them also befriended the noted Finnish architect Lars Sonck (1870–1956), who had graduated in 1894. With Finnish nationalism fueling his creative energies, Sonck subsequently made a strong impression on the three aspiring architects by designing and building an elaborate log house for himself on Finland's remote Aland Islands (situated between Finland and Sweden). Sonck's house is especially noteworthy in that it incorporated certain materials, design traits, and construction traditions common to a region on the far eastern side of Finland known as Karelia.[1]

Sonck was not alone in this pursuit of a Finnish identity but was a part of a growing movement. Although Finland had led a relatively autonomous existence since 1809, when it became a grand duchy under the control of the Russian Empire, Finns began to experience increasing oppression from the Russians during the 1890s. In an act of revolt, many artists and architects moved out of Finland's politically charged big cities, such as Turku and Helsinki, and into remote forested areas to build houses for themselves. Most of them looked to Karelia for design inspiration. The painter Axel Gallén (1865–1931; after 1907 known as Akseli Gallén-Kallela) was perhaps the most prominent among them.

The impetus behind their use of Karelia for design inspiration was *The Kalevala* (1835), a collection of Finnish epic poems that suggested to most Finns that Karelia was the home of their earliest history—the real Finland, as it were. The book had been assembled by Elias Lönnrot, a doctor who had tirelessly scoured Karelia in the late 1820s in search of such works. *The Kalevala* became Finland's national epic, harnessed by artists, architects, and designers throughout the country as both a source of inspiration for creative works and a subject of them.

Karelia, which lies on the border of Finland and Russia, extends from the coast of the White Sea in the north to the Gulf of Finland in the south and is characterized by an abundance of beautiful lakes, tiny islands, and thick forests. Despite the fact that, since the thirteenth century, the region has been subjected to numerous own-

Hvitträsk is a multi-building complex arranged around a central courtyard. This is the tower end of what is commonly referred to as the small building, the first house completed on the property. The log walls are supported by a high foundation of massive granite boulders, and the tower is finished with granite and plaster. The roof's surface material is bituminous felt.

ership battles between its residents, who were of Swedish, Finnish, and Russian descent, the Finns always managed to hold on there.[2]

The Karelian type of log house is distinguished primarily by its elaborately carved door and window surrounds and ridge-beam ornaments.[3] Because its other typical features were relatively crude, Finnish National Romantic architects and designers looked to other sources, mostly in England, for the balance of a house's design elements—form, massing, spatial plan, stylistic details, and so on. As historian Richard Weston observes, however, the overall look appeared Finnish at the time: "Recent scholarship on National Romanticism stresses the architects' manifold borrowings from international sources. In retrospect it is easy to dissect into component sources and thereby, to some extent, undermine its claims to being a peculiarly 'national' style, but its reception at the time would clearly have been rather different."[4]

Gesellius, Lindren, and Saarinen (GLS) emerged as leaders of Finland's architecture world even before they finished their schooling at the Institute. While still attending the school, in 1896, they formed their architecture practice. In 1898, the year they completed their first Karelia-inspired log house project, Villa Wuorio,[5] they won the competition to design the Finnish Pavilion at the Paris Exposition of 1900. A year later, while working on another new project, they discovered the property next to Lake Vitträsk. The construction of the monumental Hvitträsk commenced in the spring of 1902.

Hvitträsk's two primary buildings look like a castle complex as one enters the central courtyard from the winding road that leads to the property. To the left of the courtyard is the smaller, more rustic building, which was originally conceived as the residence of Gesellius, who was a bachelor at the time.[6] It is now a café—and still largely unaltered. More or less livable by August 1902, the same year GLS won the competition to design the Finnish National Museum, Saarinen stayed alone here in the second-floor room behind the gate tower while his wing of the main building, located just across the courtyard, was under construction. The spatially more complex main building, which extends in a north–south axis along a rocky promontory that overlooks the lake, was designed to accommodate living spaces for Saarinen and the Lindgren family and to house the trio's studio/office. Saarinen's two-story residence was built over a finished basement at the southern end of this building, where it was separated from the Lindgrens' residence by the centrally situated and elongated single-story studio space.

GLS's idealistic vision of a shared house/studio in the country turned out to be short-lived in practice, because the partnership began to unfold not long after Hvitträsk was completed. For reasons that remain unclear, in the spring of 1904 Saarinen alone entered and won the design competition for the Helskinki Railway Station, a move that resulted in a severe rift between himself and Lindgren and Gesellius. By the end of 1904, after living at Hvitträsk for barely a year and a half, Lindgren sold his interest in the property to Saarinen and Gesellius and headed back to Helsinki, where he lived until his death. Gesellius stayed on, however, and eventually moved out of the smaller house into Lindgren's space, which he soon

OPPOSITE, TOP Photographed from the small building, this is the front elevation of Eliel Saarinen's wing, part of the large building. It too is constructed of logs, but for reasons that remain unclear, the logs were covered with shingles in the 1910s, and these are still in place today. The tiles of the roof are mostly original.

BOTTOM Between the autumn of 1902 and the spring of 1903, while his own house was being built, Saarinen lived in the small building, in the room to the left of the tower. This house would later become the home of Saarinen's partner Herman Gesellius. The ground floor consisted of a laundry room and other service spaces, including a stable, carriage shelter, and bake house. The first floor (the second story) had two independent apartments—a single room with kitchen (about 540 square feet) at the far end of the building and, closest to the tower, a five-room arrangement with kitchen (about 1,600 square feet). These spaces remain largely unaltered, although they have been adapted for use as a restaurant.

ABOVE, LEFT This view of Saarinen's living room, shows how the bottom part of the room's walls were finished in plaster and painted. In the foreground at left, across from the stair, is one of the room's multiple built-in sofas, this one covered with an antique Finnish *ryijy* rug. The arched wall opening leads to the dining room.

RIGHT The heating stove in Saarinen's living room has an ornamental wrought-iron support at one end, a glazed brick surround, and a beautiful copper fireplace hood with floral ornamentation. Just behind the meeting table and the wrought-iron chandelier, below the row of windows, is a simple built-in sofa, also designed by Saarinen.

OPPOSITE One arrives at this point in Saarinen's living room after passing through the entry hall, which is set a few steps below this room. The Saarinens gave the living room walls an array of beautifully hand-painted ornamentation in floral motifs. This stair leads to the second-floor bedrooms and the flower room, where Loja Saarinen cultivated exotic plants.

altered to suit his own tastes. That same eventful year, Saarinen, who had recently divorced his first wife, Mathilda Gylden, married Gesellius's sister, Louise (Loja), and not long afterward Mathilda married Gesellius.

Saarinen and Gesellius remained partners until late 1907, at which time each of the architects established independent practices, although they still somehow managed to live next to each other at Hvitträsk, separated now by a solid wall that had been built in the central studio to create a formal division between their living and working spaces.

Documentation suggests that during the late 1910s portions of the exposed log walls of the main building were covered with the shingles that appear on the house today.[7] Researchers are unsure as to why this alteration was made.

After Gesellius's early death in 1916, ownership of the entire Hvitträsk estate was transferred to the Saarinens, who kept it until 1949, even though they lived in the United States for most of the year after 1923. During those years, a number of events permanently altered Hvitträsk. In the summer of 1922, two years after electricity had been installed, the tower designed by Lindgren for his wing of the house caught fire and quickly spread throughout the entire north wing of the main building. Ironically, the wall that Saarinen and Gesellius had erected in the studio, in order to separate themselves from each other, stopped the fire from reaching Saarinen's side of the studio and his house. Where the monumental north wing with its large tower once stood, Saarinen's only son, Eero (1910–1961), who would go on to worldwide acclamation for designing such works as the TWA Terminal at John F. Kennedy International Airport in New York, designed the largely unimpressive story-and-a-half house (1929–33) that is there today.

The Saarinens sold Hvitträsk to Anelma and Rainer Vuorio in 1949. Ownership of the property changed again in 1968, when it was taken over by Kansallis Osake Pankki Bank in a forced sale. A year later, tragically, most of the original furnishings, primarily works designed by Saarinen, were auctioned off, and that same year, Hvitträsk became a holding of the Gerda and Salomo Wuorio Foundation. Finally, in 1981, Hvitträsk's present owners, the Finnish government, acquired the property and painstakingly brought the buildings and landscape features back to life in order to turn the entire complex into a museum dedicated to sharing Hvitträsk with the world.

RIGHT Influenced by Charles Rennie Mackintosh's all-white Glasgow Style furniture for Hill House (1903) in Helensburgh, Scotland, Saarinen eventually designed these pieces in the "white room"—bedframe, side chairs, and vanity—for his wife. The beautifully tiled stove in the corner is not to be overlooked.

OPPOSITE Originally designed and used as a billiards room, from 1916 on this was Saarinen's library. He built the bookshelves and had the desk and chair, both dating to 1907, produced according to his designs. Many of his books and periodicals are still here.

Tallom

LOCATION
Stocksund, Sweden

YEAR BUILT
1904–6

ARCHITECT
Lars Israel Wahlman

STYLE
Norse Revival

Sited on the outskirts of Stockholm, the privately owned Tallom is one of the most important log houses in all of Sweden. The iconic form of the two-story main wing, with corbelled logs supporting the second-floor overhang, references the medieval loft house of the farms of Sweden's Dalecarlia. This is the front elevation as seen from the street. Originally, the one-story wing to the right of the entry hall's wide front door served as Lars Wahlman's design studio.

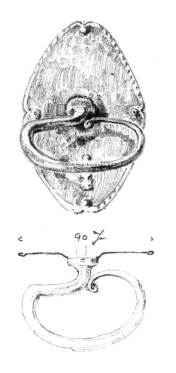

ABOVE Wahlman's pencil sketch of one of the house's door handles

OPPOSITE, TOP The first-floor, left, and second-floor plans, as prepared by Wahlman (translation: *Kök* = kitchen; *Stor-Stuga* = living room; *Forstuga* = hallway; *Spis* = fireplace; *Serv Rum* = utility room; *Matvra* = dining area; *Kämmare* = bedroom; *Jungfrukammare* = child's bedroom; *Kontor* = office; *Drängstuga* = plumbing room; *Sänkammare* = bedroom)

BOTTOM Just as in the Ornässtuga, which was Sweden's entry in the Paris Exposition of 1867 (see page 17), Tallom's second story has overhangs at the front and back. This is the first view of the house sitting atop its hilly site that one encounters after entering the neighborhood.

Situated atop its hilly site on the outskirts of Stockholm in what has become a suburban neighborhood, the monumental Tallom was conceived in 1904 as the house and studio of one of Sweden's most celebrated educators and architects, Lars Israel Wahlman (1870–1952), designer of Stockholm's landmark Engelbrekt Church (1914; masonry construction). Wahlman designed Tallom for himself while he was an instructor in the architecture division of Stockholm's Royal Institute of Technology. Although he had already seen at least twelve of his residential designs realized in various locations in Sweden since he became a professional architect in 1894, this was the first time he had ever used the log-joinery construction methods he grew up with in the Swedish province of Dalecarlia.[1] After he took up residence in the house in 1908, Wahlman wrote about its log construction in the journal *Arkitektur*: "Whether hewn or not, the walls of logs have a more truthful and honest look than any others, and no more solid wall construction can be found in the north."[2]

His decision to use this method of construction in the first house he built for himself represents more than just an expression of his personal taste. By opting to build with wood in this way, the young architect was formally aligning himself with Sweden's National Romantic movement, or more specifically with the viewpoint that the home should be a total work of art, composed of native materials such as timber and stone, built according to traditional Swedish practices dating to medieval times, and furnished primarily with items of one's own design, crafting, or manufacture. Indeed, through his writings and lectures, as well as his built works after Tallom's completion, Wahlman would come to be recognized as a leading voice of Sweden's National Romantic design movement. As historian Barbara Miller Lane observes, it was a group that subscribed to a specific methodology of design and construction: "All National Romantic architects believed . . . that a new national architecture must be derived from the earliest and simplest historic forms, which they saw as more authentic for being rooted in the earliest history of the northern peoples."[3]

Although Tallom, a house that has had the benefit of attentive care over its lifetime, is probably the best-known extant example of an architect-designed log house from this period in Sweden's history (ca. 1867–ca. 1915), it reflects the influence of several equally important, if less well known, antecedents. Among the earliest of these is a house built the year before Wahlman was born, Villa Bravalla (1869), the residence of Axel Key, a prominent professor at the Stockholm medical university, Karolinska Institutet. Miller Lane suggests that the pavilions representing Sweden and Norway at the 1867 Exposition Universelle in Paris directly inspired Villa Bravalla's design.[4] More than a decade later, the influence of these buildings could still be seen, most notably in the log-and-stave-constructed house called Storstugan II (1880) designed by Royal Academy of Fine Arts professor Carl

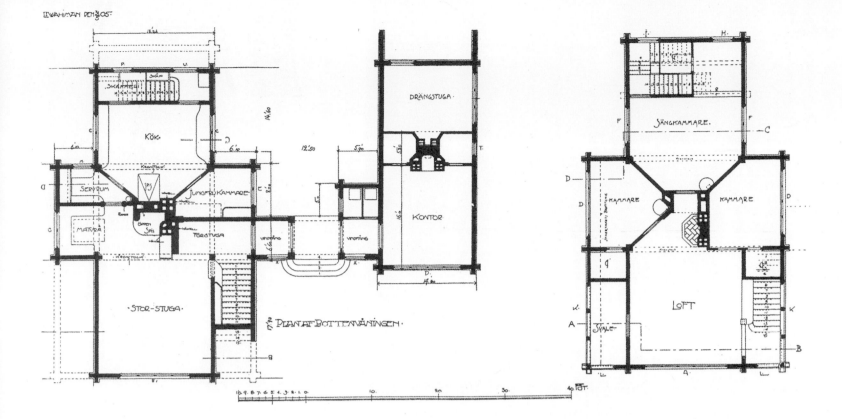

PLAN AF BOTTENVÅNINGEN.

Tallom's formal entryway, rarely used nowadays because of its distance from the driveway (hence the makeshift steps), is distinguished by this massive plank door with its original Wahlman-designed wrought-iron strap hinges, its door handle, and slender peephole. The door opens to a wide living hall.

Curman for a site in Lysekil, Sweden—the location of another Wahlman design, Villa Widmark (1902–4). The design of Storstugan II is notable for its two-story, galleried loft form.

The greatest influence on Wahlman's guiding philosophy for Tallom, however, was a group of houses that came later: the Anders Zorn home/studio complex (1887–92) and the Carl Larsson home/studio complex (1888–1912), both of which were in progress and gaining notoriety, particularly among scholars, while Wahlman was a student in architecture school. The other was Pressens Villa (1901–2), a house designed by Carl Westman (1866–1936), who was closest to Wahlman's generation. The common thread in these buildings—at least from the point of view of their exteriors—was their use of the log-construction techniques and the two-story-loft-with-cantilevered-gallery form unique to the medieval farm buildings of Dalecarlia. As Karelia was to the National Romantic architects of Finland and Zakopane to National Romantic Polish architect Stanislaw Witkiewicz during the same period, Dalecarlia represented, for Sweden's National Romantic designers, a pure source from which to mine emblems of their national identity. It was the one province in Sweden where medieval ways of life, including housing, had been the least affected by industry. Zorn and Larsson, who were both internationally famous painters, had for years been idealizing the innocent lifestyle of the Dalecarlia farmer in their work, and both had modeled their compounds of mostly log buildings on those that they had observed in Dalecarlia.[5] These images spoke to Wahlman and guided the architecture of his own house. His interiors referenced other sources, however, chief among them England's Arts and Crafts Movement, aspects of which he would have experienced at first hand during his visits to England in 1900 and 1905.

Other ideas for the three-bedroom, two-bath house and studio came from Wahlman's studies of various buildings that had been moved from Dalecarlia and other rural locations to Stockholm's open-air museum called Skansen, which had opened a decade earlier, in 1891. In his only book, *Verk Av L I Wahlman,* which includes some English translations, he speaks of measuring and researching in particular "the leaky Dalecarlia cottages at Skansen"[6] in order to know what not to do in the construction of Tallom. The accompanying drawings illustrate the solutions he would ultimately devise and utilize in the creation of this building, which is still structurally impeccable a century later.

Wahlman lived and worked in Tallom until his death in 1952, all the while using it as a showcase of his design philosophy and a laboratory for his ideas. As he put it:

"The dry security of my wooden walls is indicative more of common sense than of poetry. But Tallom and Norhaga [a Wahlman-designed house of ca. 1903–7 for Lars Yngström, near Falun, Sweden] stand solitary. They too must have poetry, a belief in a Sweden sane and sound."[7] His neighbors in Stocksund must have received Tallom warmly, since almost immediately after its completion in 1906 Wahlman was commissioned to design other houses there, including Villa Lindström (1906–7) and Villa von Greyerz (1907–9).

After Wahlman's death, Tallom went through several hands before being acquired in 1975 by its current owners, Olaf Karlander and Marie G. Dotter Hafström. Alterations to the original design have been minimal; only the kitchen, which was expanded at the back in the 1960s to accommodate the installation of modern appliances, differs markedly from what it was when Wahlman was last here.

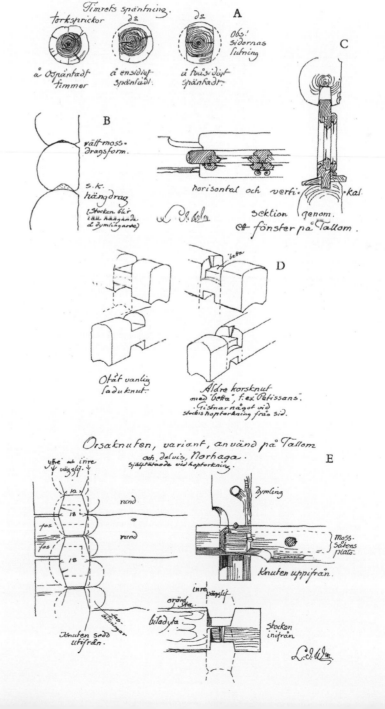

ABOVE The brown-stained log walls of Tallom are masterfully constructed in full-scribe joinery with locking corners and feature elaborate, carved ornamentation highlighted in red stain.

RIGHT Accompanying this drawing of log-construction details by Walhman, which appeared in a 1908 edition of the journal *Arkitektur*, is the following text, which is keyed to the illustrations.

A. The timber dries more quickly when hewn on two sides.

B. The groove was made somewhat deeper than the curve of the log below. Additional packing has never been done or needed.

C. If the lower member of the frame reaches the bottom of its groove, the upper member must have a groove large enough to allow for settling.

D. This type of log construction is still well known to the traditional Dalecarlia carpenters and can be found in many old cottages in southern Dalecarlia. The Tallom joints, developed after much measuring and research among the leaky Dalecarlia cottages at Skansen (an open-air museum in Stockholm), were something of a novelty for these skilled carpenters.

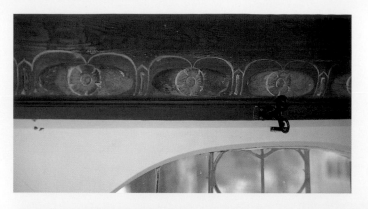

TOP Instead of curtains or other kinds of window treatments, Wahlman gave the areas around each window elaborate carvings, each painted by hand. "The timbered house lends itself well to carving," he wrote in 1908, "and there is no difficulty in choosing places for decoration. A wavy line around windows and doors helps to take us away from the rags of curtains, a plain sign of degeneration, and from the lining pieces those rags are meant to conceal."

LEFT More carved-and-painted ornamentation can be found on the timber post of the stairway that leads to the second-floor loft. In the background is a door that leads to the living hall, which separates the house from the studio.

RIGHT The first-floor living room, situated in the front part of the two-story wing, just past the fireplace and dining nook, is one of the few rooms whose log walls were spared latex paint. Notice the abundance of carved ornamentation around the windows, from which curtains were deliberately omitted.

TOP, LEFT The kitchen has been modernized but still has its wood-burning oven.

TOP, RIGHT Wahlman designed built-in seating for the dining nook, which is open to the living room. The floral ornamentation on the fireplace is noteworthy for its level of detail. The door in the center of the photograph leads to the kitchen.

RIGHT The second-floor loft is situated at the front of the house, just above the living room. In the decades since Wahlman's death, the owners of the house have painted the log walls and other wood surfaces.

Clubhouse, Stickley Museum at Craftsman Farms

LOCATION
Morris Plains, New Jersey

YEAR BUILT
1911

DESIGNER
Gustav Stickley

BUILDER
Craftsman Home Builders Club

STYLE
Craftsman

Nearly a century after Gustav Stickley (1858–1946) first bought property in Morris Plains, the skyscrapers and the congestion of nearby Newark and New York City still seem a world away as one enters the winding road that stems from the highway into the uninterrupted tranquility of Craftsman Farms. This is what initially drew Stickley to the place, of course, and ultimately compelled him to acquire about 650 acres in the town.

America's most prominent voice in the Arts and Crafts Movement would use this land as the location of his own planned community—a family residence, farm, school, and workshop complex—all in keeping with the back-to-nature philosophy of living espoused by his magazine *The Craftsman* (183 issues published between 1901 and 1916). Along the way, however, the self-made German-American entrepreneur from Wisconsin saw his vast real-estate holdings and businesses in furniture design and manufacture, magazine and book publishing, and residential design and construction become an overwhelming financial burden. In his attempts to create a Craftsman empire, Stickley had grown too fast. In 1915, with his base of operations occupying all twelve stories of the prominent Craftsman Building at 6 East Thirty-ninth Street in Manhattan, Stickley declared bankruptcy, a situation from which he would never recover.[1]

Although he was never able to realize his entire plan, Stickley did manage to construct on the farm a few shingled cottages and, most notably, the Clubhouse.[2] Designed in 1908 and completed in 1911, the Clubhouse is the most compelling building at Craftsman Farms and the only one of log construction. When it was published in his book *More Craftsman Homes* (1912), Stickley described its site and its construction of chestnut logs: "As in the pioneer days, the space for this house had first to be cleared in the forest. The abundant chestnut trees were cut down and of them the house is built. The logs are hewn on two sides and peeled and the hewn sides laid together and chinked with cement mortar. The logs are stained the color of the bark."[3]

Stickley's motivation for constructing in logs, a topic he elaborated on at length in his essay "Architectural Development of the Log Cabin in America,"[4] is rooted in the then-widespread romantic perception of the log cabin as the original American house.[5] Furthermore, like his Craftsman furniture, the house built of logs epitomized structural honesty and, more than any other common house type, suggested a certain in-harmony-with-nature ideal. As an ardent advocate of simplicity and honesty in design and construction, Stickley placed enormous value on the image of the simple pioneer dwelling made of materials found on site.

Given the resources at his disposal as the owner of a residential design and construction company, Stickley could have constructed the main building at Craftsman Farms in any number of ways, but he chose log construction. "To us in America the

The side of Stickley's house, with the full-width enclosed porch—what he called the "piazza"—is the most attractive of the exteriors.

log cabin seems a dear friend," Stickley wrote. "What a train of historical reminiscence the mere thought of the log cabin awakens: the landing of the first settlers, the unbroken wilderness of the primeval forests, the clearing of the ground, the building of the first homes."[6]

Stickley's reflections on the log house in *More Craftsman Homes* demonstrate clearly that he had become caught up in what historian Harold R. Shurtleff later termed "the log cabin myth." Still, no matter what his motivations were for adopting it, the log house received a boost from its associations with Stickley.[7] After all, Stickley was the first high-profile American designer to suggest publicly, in both his books and his periodicals, the idea of the log house's potential as legitimate high-art architecture. In the essay quoted above, he even suggests that—in the stylistic manner in which he had recast it (the Craftsman mode)—the log house could serve as America's national house type: "Since the log house has played so important a part in our history, its development into a definite and characteristic type of architecture might give us something national, something peculiarly American in suggestiveness."[8]

Although the Stickleys lived in the Clubhouse during their years at the farm, it was not originally intended as their residence. Indeed, as the building's less-than-domestic scale and awkwardly attached kitchen wing suggests, it was designed to be a public space, a gathering place for the farm's owner, employees, students, and guests. In the October 1908 issue of *The Craftsman*, Stickley published a drawing of the house he had intended to build for himself,[9] but the two-and-a-half-story, half-timbered design of German influence never materialized beyond the pages of the magazine. Instead Stickley opted to make certain revisions to the Clubhouse plan so that it would accommodate his family, if only temporarily, although the family continued to live there until they lost the farm to bankruptcy in 1915. Two years later, the bank sold Craftsman Farms to Major George Farny for $100,000.[10]

The Farny family maintained the buildings until the late 1980s. When in 1987 it appeared that the buildings of Craftsman Farms would be demolished to make way for a developer's townhouse complex, the township of Parsippany-Troy Hills rallied and stepped in to save the property. Now in their ownership and a designated National Historic Landmark, the twenty-six-acre Stickley Museum at Craftsman Farms, including the Clubhouse, is open to the public and is dedicated to promoting the continued relevance of the Arts and Crafts Movement in the United States and the ideas of Gustav Stickley.

"Stickley's vision," says Hewitt, "proved more durable than the dreams of many Arts and Crafts proponents; his buildings, landscapes, and artifacts continue to provide lessons to those people who would remake the world as a sustainable environment, as a place where art and life may be united under the ideal of craftsmanship."[11]

BELOW According to Stickley's instructions, the chestnut logs were hewn (on the tops and bottoms only) and then peeled and stained a color resembling the chestnut bark before being stacked and chinked with cement mortar. The logs are joined with a pegged lap joint. That he did not choose the more refined dovetail or tooth-notch joinery methods is surprising, particularly in light of the impeccable joinery techniques and overall craftsmanship of his furniture. One might say the log construction of the Clubhouse is a reflection of Stickley's romantic affinity for the log cabins of the American pioneer.

OPPOSITE Technically, this is the front of the house. The formal entrance is the doorway at the far right side of the photograph, in what was originally the kitchen. The chimneys are made of stones gathered from the site.

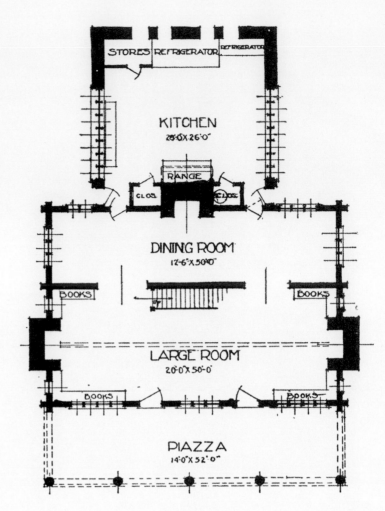

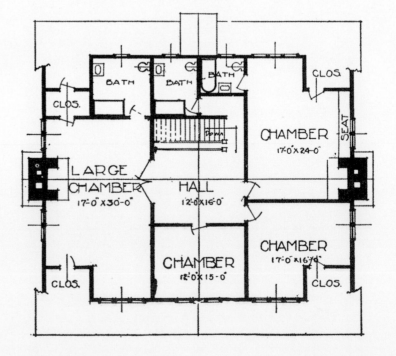

TOP The awkwardness of the first-floor spatial arrangement reveals the originally intended use of the house as a place for public gatherings and for housing guests.

BOTTOM The second-floor plan, for some reason, clusters all of the bathrooms, one next to the other.

OPPOSITE Besides being of great interest as the log home of America's leader of the Arts and Crafts movement, the significance of the Clubhouse becomes apparent when one enters the interior. The Craftsman furnishings, many of which are original to the house, work beautifully within the exposed log architecture. This is one end of what the plan calls the "large room," an area that is 20 feet deep by about 50 feet wide. Its fireplaces, one at each end, have deep, tiled hearths below large copper hoods that have inscriptions. This one reads: "By hammer and hand do all things stand."

OPPOSITE The middle section of the large room has an opening that connects it with the dining room and, further back, the kitchen. Here we also see a close-up of the network of peeled chestnut logs that support the ceiling. The two lamps hanging from the log capital of the post in the foreground are Stickley designs, original to the house.

RIGHT This view is from the fireplace across to the other side of the large room. The piazza is situated to the left.

Power House

LOCATION
Wolf Creek, Montana

YEAR BUILT
1913

ARCHITECTS
Robert C. Reamer, William E. Donovan

STYLE
Craftsman

The setting of the Power House is spectacular and highly secluded. From the highway, a long bumpy dirt road leads to the base of a mountainous granite outcropping. This side of the house is near the far back end of the property. As at Stickley's Clubhouse, the logs of the first floor on this side are left exposed, while those of the second-floor are sheathed in cedar shakes. In this instance, the effect, which is purely decorative, suggests half-timbering. The stones of the chimneystacks, restored in 2003 (using the same stones), were taken from the outcropping behind the house.

In the United States of 1910, the bungalow type of residence was well on its way to becoming a ubiquitous presence on the nation's landscape, no longer just an attractive option for a summer house. Frequently promoted by editors of such magazines as Good Housekeeping, Ladies' Home Journal, Gustav Stickley's *The Craftsman,* and Bungalow Magazine, this humble house type of Anglo-Indian origin was typically characterized by a squat story-and-one-half shape, broad roof overhangs, exposed and decorated rafter tails, multiple porches, and an open plan with rooms featuring built-in storage and seating areas. It also found an enthusiastic audience through plan books, including Stickley's Craftsman Homes (1909), and mail-order catalogues, such as those issued by Sears Roebuck. "For as little as $5," observes historian Diane Maddex, "would-be homeowners could purchase complete sets of plans and specifications and erect the bungalow of their choice. With few exceptions, these bungalows came from the drawing boards of anonymous architects."[1]

In 1910 Charles B. Power, a prominent businessman in Helena, Montana, was planning a house for his ranch in Wolf Creek some thirty-five miles north of town, and for him the bungalow was an ideal choice, although he wanted an especially rustic version built of logs. For a man of Power's status (his father, T. C. Power, had served as a United States Senator from Montana), an anonymous architect would not suffice. He insisted on hiring the country's most accomplished designer of rustic buildings, Robert C. Reamer (1873–1938), the architect of the Old Faithful Inn (1903), a log-shingle-and-stone spectacle at Yellowstone National Park.

In December 1910, Power sent a letter to Reamer asking if he would be interested in designing the house. Within a few days, Reamer, who was then at Yellowstone monitoring the construction of his seven-hundred-room Grand Canyon Hotel (1911),[2] responded: "I have your letter of Dec. 1st, about a log bungalow at your ranch. I would be very much pleased to make these plans for you in any state of completion that you may wish them."[3] In addition to providing a quote of $175 for "detail plans and specifications," Reamer suggested that, although it would be at least three months before he would be able to travel to Helena (ostensibly to see the site and oversee the construction), he would be willing to create drawings, which he would submit to Power by mail. Power consented to Reamer's terms, and the process, much of which can be pieced together today from the surviving correspondence between architect and client, was soon under way.

On February 7, 1911, Reamer revealed his proposed design to Power, sending to him by registered mail a sketch accompanied by a letter explaining the design decisions he had made. Although it was to be built at least partially of logs, the house depicted in the drawing resembled a common ranch-type house, a building with pronounced utilitarian connotations, rather than a bungalow. "You will notice that I

ABOVE This view, captured from the approach to the house, highlights the Power House's imposing jerkinhead gable roof, exposed log purlins, and second-floor porch with Adirondack Style bracing in the balustrade. Here the log construction, all of it finished with a brown creosote stain, is exposed through to the roof. The shakes seen on the opposite gable end are here used only on the walls of the porch enclosure. The bargeboards, again as in Stickley's house, are unornamented. The house's porte cochère is at the far right side in the photograph.

OPPOSITE It is unusual to find the correspondence between the architect and the owner of a house almost a century old so carefully archived. The Power family retained these insightful documents and passed them on to the O'Connells, the second and present owners, when the house was sold. Reproduced here is the first letter from architect Robert Reamer to C. B. Power, a response to Power's request for consultation.

have made the entire building on one floor," Reamer wrote in the letter, "for the reason that I did not think you would be satisfied with the appearance had the kitchen part been made two stories and the main building one story. Furthermore, the more ground a building of this character covers the better it will look."[4]

On February 24, 1911, Reamer sent Power another letter informing him that he would soon be sending the floor plans by express mail. He itemized the materials needed for the building, a total of 446 logs of varying lengths and "sized top and bottom to 10 inches" so they "will lay flat and leave no large crack."[5]

The month of March came and went, and despite his earlier promises to the contrary, Reamer still had not made it to the Wolf Creek site. More letters were exchanged, and Reamer explained that the Grand Canyon Hotel project would occupy him at least until July 1.[6] Power eventually tired of waiting for Reamer, and in August he took the plans he had bought from Reamer to the architecture firm of Donovan & Rhoads, which was based not far away, in the city of Great Falls. Principal architect William E. Donovan took over the project and transformed the single-story, log-and-shingle ranch house with its I-shape plan into the two-story, rectangle-shape log bungalow that Power had presumably been seeking all along. He did, however, adopt certain rustic interior details that Reamer had conceived for the house.

YELLOWSTONE PARK HOTEL CO.

YELLOWSTONE PARK, WYO.

Dec. 5, 1910.

Mr. C. B. Power,
Helena, Mont.

Dear Sir:

I have your letter of Dec. 1st, about a log bungalow at your ranch. I would be very much pleased to make these plans for you in any state of completion that you may wish them.

For your guidance in this matter, I might say that my charges for a sketch of the exterior and sketch-plan which would be sent to you for your approval and alteration before going further, together with scale plans and elevations with sufficient descriptions for a building of this character, would be $100.00. If you should wish complete detail plans and specifications, such as you would require if contracting in a city, it would be $175.00. However, I think the latter for a building of this character unnecessary. The former would denote the plan and length of logs, size of windows, doors, and if you wish it, a complete lumber list.

I hardly think I will be in Helena for some time, possibly in March. If this should be too late, you might send me whatever information you may have, that is if you wish me to go on with this matter, and I will work up a sketch, submitting it to you through the mail.

Yours truly,

Robert C. Reamer

RCR RMS

In early 1913, the construction of the Power House was finally completed, for a total of $12,000.[7] Power then hired the prestigious firm of Marshall Field & Company of Chicago to supply custom-made rustic lighting fixtures for each room. That year, the *Great Falls Tribune* declared the Power House "the best country residence in Montana, if not in the Northwest."

The Power family retained ownership of the property for the next three decades, eventually selling the ranch and house in 1946 to Brian O'Connell, a local rancher and the Lewis and Clark County sheriff. The idea of selling the house, as Pat O'Connell Anderson, O'Connell's daughter and current owner of the house, points out, did not find favor with Power's wife, Pauline: "Mrs. Power was angry about giving up the house. She had left it in pretty rough shape, in protest it seemed, and she took with her a number of the original fixtures that belonged to the house."[8] In 1969, after Pauline Power's death, the Power family held an estate sale, where the O'Connells found and finally reclaimed the items she had taken from the house in 1946.

Today the O'Connell family operates the Power House as a hotel. Called Bungalow Bed and Breakfast, the National Historic Landmark is a favorite destination for aficionados of bungalows and the Craftsman Style. Thanks to the O'Connells' meticulous care, the four-bedroom house has undergone only the most exacting restoration work and is very much the same house that was built in 1913.

Although the finished design differs markedly from what Reamer had originally proposed, visitors to the house find his influence unmistakable. As historian Ruth Quinn points out, "One cannot experience the interior without being transported in spirit to Reamer's Old Faithful Inn."[9]

ABOVE The house's doorframes have been deftly fitted into the Idaho cedar log courses. The patina on the peeled logs is the result of the owner's thorough biannual application of Old English Red Cedar Oil.
RIGHT The porte cochère has the massive stone piers that are common in bungalow design across the United States. Note how the stonework was handled in order to accommodate the diagonal log bracing.

OPPOSITE The living room, which is open to the second floor, is at the center of the house and has 22-foot ceilings and a monumental granite fireplace with 6-by-6-inch clay tiles in the wide hearth. Built-in window seats flank the fireplace, and two skylights were recently added above the hearth area. The dining room is to the left of the stair that leads to the loft side of the second floor.

ABOVE The dining room has oak floors and beaverboard ceilings, like the rest of the house. Note the clean, uniform application of the chinking.

OPPOSITE The second-floor loft's log post-and-beam structure recalls the old log-constructed lodges of the National Park system. The lighting—each piece an original—was custom made for the house by Marshall Field & Company of Chicago.

Semmering House

LOCATION
Semmering, Austria

YEAR BUILT
Unbuilt (designed 1913)

ARCHITECT
Adolf Loos

STYLE
Heimatstil / Craftsman

TOP Original elevation of one side of Loos's Semmering House. The American Craftsman Style design details are clearly indicated in this rendering.
BOTTOM This section drawing, prepared by Ludwig Münz, illustrates Loos's Raumplan concept of varying room heights according to function. In an interview from 1930, he commented on it specifically: "For me, there is no ground floor, first floor etc. . . . For me, there are only contiguous, continual spaces, rooms, anterooms, terraces etc. Storeys merge and spaces relate to each other. Every space requires a different height: the dining room is surely higher than the pantry, thus the ceilings are set at different levels. To join these spaces in such a way that the rise and fall are not only unobservable but also practical, in this I see what is for others the great secret, although it is for me a great matter of course."

"Architecture arouses moods in people, so the task of the architect is to give these moods concrete expression. A room must look cozy, a house comfortable to live in."[1] This rational view was offered in 1910 by Viennese journalist, architect, and educator Adolf Loos (1870–1933) in an article in the Berlin periodical *Der Sturm*. In spite of this warm sentiment, Loos's prominent role in the history of the early Modern movement in architecture is to a large degree based on an essay he had written in 1908 entitled "Ornament und Verbrechen" (Ornament and Crime), in which he railed with characteristic lucidity against the abuse of ornament in architecture, a notion dramatically realized in 1910 in his Villa Steiner in Vienna. This innovative building was a radically minimalist design of reinforced concrete (one of the earliest examples) painted bright white and capped by an arched sheet-metal roof—all completely bare, free of ornamentation.

Even today, in spite of the fact that the Modern movement has gained widespread acceptance, not to mention that we have been conditioned by nearly a century of technological progress, Loos's Villa Steiner, which was regarded as cutting edge for its time, still fails to look "comfortable to live in." Such a contradiction is not uncommon, however, in the three decades of work produced by this unquestionably brilliant man. Many who know of his polemics and his built work would never suspect him of having designed a log house, but in fact he did just that.

Loos spent most of his life in Vienna, although that did not get in the way of his preoccupation with the United States. In *Adolf Loos on Architecture* (1995), contributors Adolf and Daniel Opel suggest that, throughout his life, Loos "remained convinced of the absolute superiority of the English and American lifestyle." In the dozens of articles that Loos wrote in which America was in one way or another held up as an example for his readers to follow, he was speaking from personal experience. He had traveled to the United States in 1893, shortly after completing his formal design training at the Technical School in Dresden, Germany. After arriving in America, Loos headed straight for Chicago's Jackson Park to visit the World's Columbian Exposition. He remained in the United States for the next three years, traveling to St. Louis, Philadelphia, and New York and sustaining himself by working a variety of construction jobs, before he eventually returned to Vienna to pursue his design ambitions.[2]

Perhaps it was Loos's affinity for the United States that provoked him in 1913—at the height of the Craftsman Movement in America—to design the log-constructed Semmering House as he did. Drawings for the unbuilt project were made during the time when he was operating his own architecture school, the Adolf Loos School of Building, in a space provided for him by the Schwarzwald School in Vienna. The house was commissioned by one of the school's staff members for a sloping site in Semmering, Austria, a stunning alpine town about fifty-six miles outside Vienna.

PLAN ZVR ERRICHTVNG
EINER BAVLEITVNGSHVTTE
FVR DIE SEMMERINGSCHVLE

MASSTAB 1:100

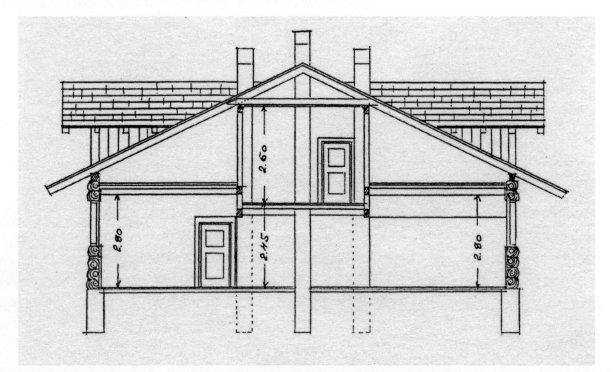

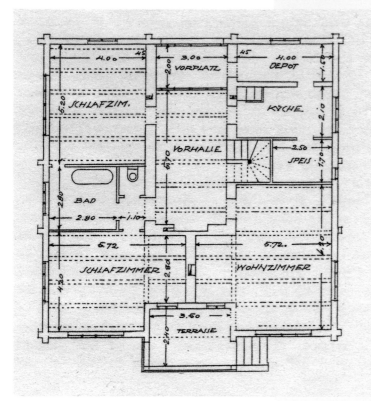

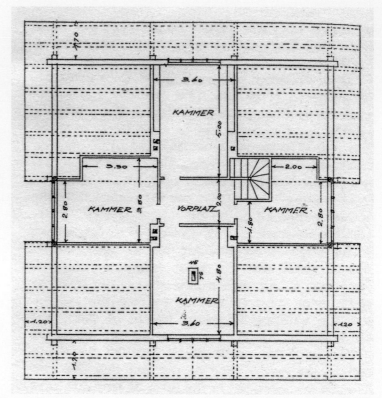

LEFT The first-floor plan, also by Münz, illustrating how Loos has the front entry situated off a porch that opens to the living room (translation: *Kammer* = room; *Vorplatz* = landing or hall; *Schlafzimmer* = bedroom; *Vorhalle* = hall; *Kuche* = kitchen; *Speis* = dining area; *Wohnzimmer* = living room; *Terrasse* = porch).

RIGHT The second-floor plan

At least three decades earlier, Semmering's tranquil beauty had been discovered by Viennese high society as an ideal location in which to build a country getaway cottage or villa. By the late 1890s, the once sparsely populated area saw new construction become widespread, most of it residential and built to designs by leading Viennese architects.[3] For its prominent role in establishing what in subsequent decades became the Semmering country-house design vernacular—what is often referred to as Heimatstil (Homeland Style)—the 1894 villa of noted Viennese architect Franz von Neumann should be seen as one of the most important of these early houses.[4] Although Neumann's design alludes to certain Swiss-farmhouse influences, on the whole it typifies the commonly held image of the pre-twentieth-century Austrian country house, complete with its *Blockhaus*-type log construction (the ground floor clad in whitewashed plaster, the second and third floors left exposed and fronted by elaborately detailed balconies) and its overall emphasis on verticality. For the Schwarzwald staff member's house, a modest project for the area, Loos ignored much of this historicism.

His Semmering House design suggests a pared-down American Craftsman bungalow more than it resembles an Austrian Heimatstil cottage. Although the broad overhangs and prominently exposed rafter tails of the roof are major characteristics of both styles, the generally squat form of the Semmering House, with its front-facing gabled roof of moderate pitch and low eaves, are pure Craftsman. Loos published sympathetic views of England's Arts and Crafts Movement on more than one occasion, but it is not known whether or not he followed its American offshoot led by Gustav Stickley (1858–1942). Stickley's Craftsman Style architecture had been widely promoted by 1913, certainly enough for news of it to have reached Vienna and the receptive Loos. Unfortunately, there is not much information in the Loos archives about this particular project.[5]

During the same year that he designed the log house, Loos published his "Rules for Building in the Mountains," a set of principles that still bear some relevance today, almost a century later:

> Take note of the forms in which the country folk build. They are wisdom from our forefathers, essence made manifest. But seek the reason for the form. If technical advance has made it possible to improve the form, then the improvement is always to be used. The flail is replaced by the threshing machine.
>
> Do not think about the roof, but about rain and snow. That is how the country folk think and why in the mountains they give their roofs the shallowest pitch their technical experience tells them is possible. In the mountains the snow should not slide off whenever it feels like it, but when the inhabitants want. For that reason they must be able to climb up on the roof without endangering their lives to get rid of the snow. And we should create the shallowest roof possible according to our technical experience.
>
> Do not be afraid to be criticized for being old-fashioned. Changes in the old way of building are permissible only when they are improvements. Otherwise stick to things as they always have been. For truth, even if it be hundreds of years old, has a closer connection with our inner being than the untruth marching along beside us.[6]

Some sixteen years after designing in logs for the Schwarzwald School's staff member, a log-house design by Loos was in fact realized in Semmering. Completed three years before the architect's death, for a client who had first hired him in 1907 to renovate an apartment in Vienna, the Khuner House (1930) pays homage to the Heimatstil, at least in its form and method of construction. Like so many *Blockhaus* buildings found throughout the mountains of Austria, Khuner House's vertically oriented rectangle shape rests on a stone foundation and is sheltered under a broad single-gable roof with moderate pitch and eaves that reach out several feet beyond the house's side walls. The front elevation has a second-floor balcony, another char-

The Khuner House, built in 1930, is another log-house design by Loos, one that was in fact realized in Semmering.

acteristic feature. It becomes obvious that the house was designed by a Modernist, however, when one considers its highly progressive window arrangement and the lack of exterior ornament. The double-height sitting room, which one enters through the front door, receives light through a wide two-story window. There are no decorative bargeboards or carvings around this opening, or any of the others, however. Plain, sliding shutters, set vertically in some places and horizontally in others, make it possible to seal the house off easily from harsh weather.

Khuner House, the only building by the architect to feature *Blockhaus* construction, has been hailed as a masterpiece.[7] It is now operated as a hotel and restaurant called Loos Haus.

Log House

LOCATION
Unknown

YEAR DESIGNED
Unbuilt (designed 1916–18)

ARCHITECT
Rudolf M. Schindler

STYLE
Prairie

The year was 1915, and a young Viennese draftsman named Rudolf Schindler (1887–1953) was seated on a train watching the American West fly by. The trip, a late-summer vacation from his recently landed job with the Chicago architecture firm of Ottenheimer, Stern, and Reichel (OSR), marked the first time he had ever been out West, and it would take him through Colorado, New Mexico, Arizona, Utah, and California. Schindler was equipped with a sketchbook and a new Kodak camera, and both would receive a good deal of use, especially during his visits to the south rim of the Grand Canyon; various parts of Taos, where he became enamored of the area's Pueblo-inspired adobe design and construction; and the Pan Pacific Expositions in San Francisco and San Diego, where architecture was given special emphasis.[1]

At the Grand Canyon Schindler would no doubt have encountered the very prominently sited and actively promoted El Tovar Hotel (1905), a sprawling one-hundred-room log spectacle designed by Chicago architect Charles F. Whittlesey (1867–1941). Whittlesey's El Tovar, a frame structure covered with log-slab siding, was an elegant building, yet appropriately rustic for its forested site, which had by this time become a focal point of the park and a much sought-after destination for tourists from all over the world.[2] In addition to El Tovar, dramatically perched about twenty-five feet from the sharp edge of the south rim of the Canyon was the double-pen[3] William "Buckey" O'Neill Cabin (1890s), a structure built entirely of logs by O'Neill himself. It too would have caught Schindler's eye, even if its architectural modesty did not inspire him. He may also have seen Hermit's Rest (1914), the latest building by the Grand Canyon's head architect and designer, Mary Colter (1869–1958). Hermit's Rest had been constructed of local stone and logs, and its interior was characterized by peeled log walls and beams that protruded forcefully from the building's façade.

At the Pan Pacific Expositions of 1915–16, held simultaneously in San Diego, San Francisco, and Seattle in celebration of the opening of the Panama Canal, the dominant architectural themes were Mission Revival and Spanish Colonial Revival. At the San Francisco fair, however, rustic architecture made at least one noteworthy appearance: Bernard Maybeck's House of Hoo Hoo. Composed of massive tree trunks, the house is likely to have caught Schindler's attention.

After returning to Chicago from his vacation travels and resuming his duties at OSR, Schindler began to work on a number of small side projects. One of these, begun in 1916, was this flat-roofed modular log house, his first from-the-ground-up exercise in Frank Lloyd Wright's Prairie Style mode.[4] The Prairie Style, introduced in a 1901 *Ladies Home Journal* article entitled "A Small House in a Prairie Town," was Wright's proposal for a truly American style of architecture. Its strong horizontal lines—in particular its low-pitched roofs with extended overhangs and bands of

Schindler's side elevations show the flat-roofed log house floating over stone piers. Note the clerestory windows with wood shutters positioned beneath the protruding log ends of the roof structure.

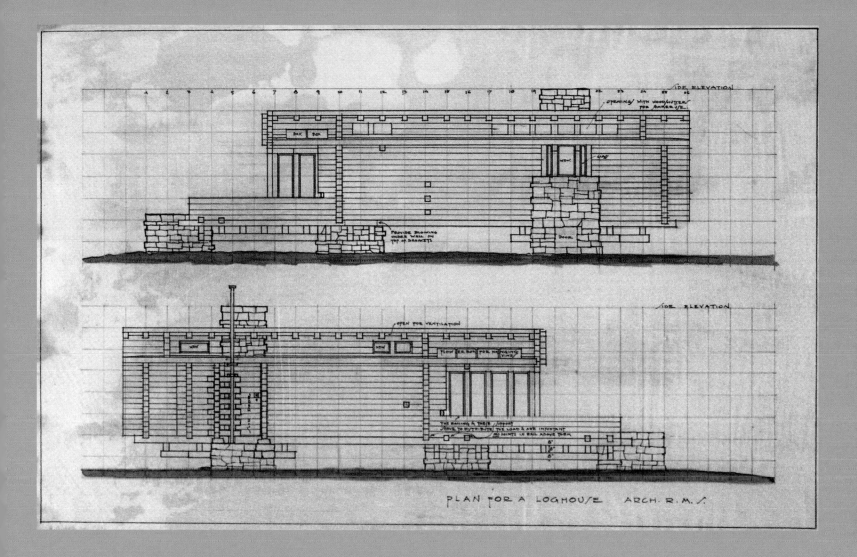

PLAN FOR A LOGHOUSE   ARCH. R. M. S.

windows—appeared to hug the flat Midwestern landscape from which the style had drawn inspiration. For the better part of the three decades that followed, referring to Wright's thoroughly publicized prototypes such as the Fricke House, the Willits House, and the Robie House (each in the vicinity of Chicago and dating to 1901–2), architects and builders installed thousands of Prairie Style houses in suburbs across the United States. Log construction is not known to have been a component of these buildings, however. Schindler's opting to design a Prairie Style log house is therefore somewhat perplexing—perhaps the most unusual project in his oeuvre.

Schindler wanted nothing more than to work under Wright, the outspoken American architect whose monograph *The Wasmuth Portfolio* (1910) he had spent so much time admiring as a student at the Vienna Academy of Arts. After all, it was because of Wright that he had been interested in relocating to Chicago in the first place. In 1917, after a number of unsuccessful attempts, Schindler finally went to work for his idol. When he arrived at Wright's office, numerous Prairie Style houses for sites in the United States were on Wright's drafting boards or in construction, along with the project that commanded most of Wright's attention, the Imperial Hotel for Tokyo (1915–19). Soon Schindler found himself directly involved in the design and engineering of several of these buildings. For the time being, the Log House drawings would have to be put aside.

In February 1918, Wright relocated Schindler and the rest of his staff to Spring Green, Wisconsin, where his land and complex of buildings called Taliesin was located. There Schindler worked on the Imperial Hotel project in earnest. It was about this time that he revisited the Log House project. The final drawings for the house—which are in the Schindler Archives and are reproduced here—date from this period. Sadly, little else is on record other than what the drawings themselves reveal, so we are unable to determine if the Log House project evolved into a Prairie Style house because of Wright's influence or if it had been originally conceived as such.

Schindler remained at Taliesin until 1920, the year Wright moved him to Hollywood, California, to supervise the construction of a multi-building residential project. After settling in Hollywood, Schindler began to build a house of his own there, the concrete-walled, outdoors-embracing Schindler-Chase House (1921–22). This progressive, seminal work had the effect of establishing Schindler as an early proponent of the Modern scene that was about to blossom in southern California. Working from his house in Hollywood, Schindler would become one of Modernism's most prolific forces, ultimately designing more than 500 buildings, of which about 150 were built, and achieving the icon status that is bestowed upon him today. He remained a resident of Los Angeles until his final days.

Schindler's Log House, in addition to being a genuine curiosity, is the earliest-known example of a log house designed in a Modern idiom in America or anywhere else. As such, it holds a place of importance in the storyline of the high-art log house.

TOP The window arrangement recalls that of Frank Lloyd Wright's Willits House (1901) in Highland Park, Illinois.

BOTTOM Schindler's notes include his specification that all of logs for the house are to be hewn only on the tops and bottoms for stacking purposes. Even more interesting is his allusion to using logs for "interior furniture." Note the drawings that illustrate how he intended to stack and join the logs.

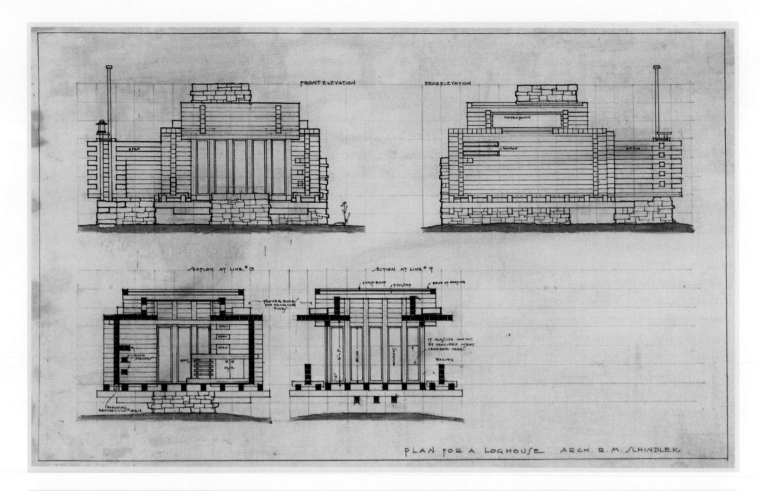

FRONT ELEVATION   REAR ELEVATION

SECTION AT LINE #13   SECTION AT LINE #9

PLAN FOR A LOGHOUSE   ARCH. R.M. SCHINDLER

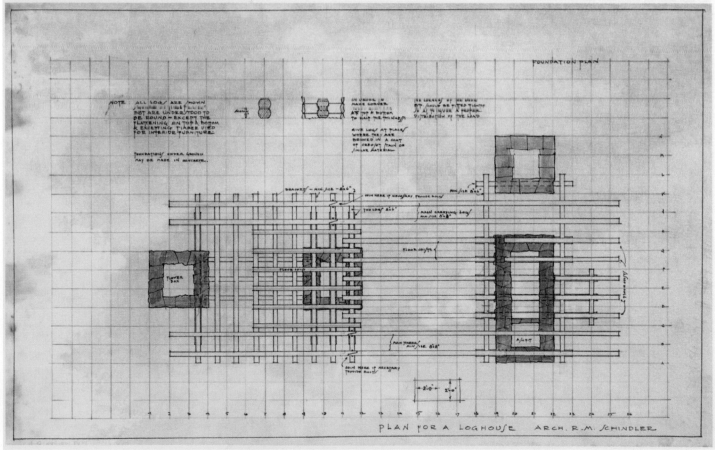

FOUNDATION PLAN

PLAN FOR A LOGHOUSE   ARCH. R.M. SCHINDLER

Villa Vekara

LOCATION
Karstula, Finland

YEAR BUILT
1924

ARCHITECT
Alvar Aalto

STYLE
Nordic Classicism

This side elevation of Villa Vekara reveals the volume of the small house and its overall asymmetrical character—in particular the roof and the arrangement of the windows. The house's many traditional Finnish farmhouse characteristics (such as the exposed hewn logs with the board-and-batten cladding and the high-relief white-painted window frames with drip cap) are easily recognized after one studies the old log houses on display at the Seurasaari Open-Air Museum in Helsinki. In Vekara Aalto has put a high-art spin on an old Finnish vernacular form.

Along with Frank Lloyd Wright, Mies van der Rohe, and Le Corbusier, Alvar Aalto (1898–1976) of Finland is one of the most widely recognized figures in the world of Modernist architecture and design. Because of his still-popular line of wood furniture for Artek and his signature buildings—which include the Tuberculosis Sanatorium (1929–33) in Paimio, Finland; Villa Mairea (1938) in Noormarkku, Finland; the Finnish Pavilion at the New York World's Fair (1939); the Cultural Center (1955–58) in Helsinki; and the Opera House (1959) in Essen, Germany—there is today an international awareness of Aalto's enormous contributions. Certainly it is greater than that of his primary teacher, Armas Lindgren, whose work in log construction is also featured in this book (see page 48). Although it is not generally considered his primary area of expertise, Aalto designed about one hundred single-family houses, half of which were realized, during the course of his long career from 1921 to 1976. Many of these houses are located in Finland, and several of them—most notably Villa Mairea, now a museum—include elaborate sauna buildings, which according to Finnish custom were of log construction with a sod roof.[1]

In the typical Finnish farmstead of old, the first building to be constructed was usually the sauna. It still holds greater value in Finnish culture than any other building type. Besides bathing, Finns have traditionally used saunas for a multitude of purposes, such as conducting important business discussions and social gatherings. Many Finns were born in a sauna—a building that has a naturally sterile environment. That Aalto also designed a number of single-family houses featuring exposed log construction is, unfortunately, a little-known aspect of his distinguished career, overshadowed by his many large-scale works.

To these single-family log houses in the Aalto oeuvre—each a beautiful design whose measured drawings, preserved in the Aalto archives, could inspire the building of a log house today—may be added many prefab-housing designs that featured exposed pine-log construction and sod roofs.[2] In too many instances, both types of structures have been lost—destroyed by fire or demolished to make way for new developments. As we discovered during our long journey through Finland looking for privately owned Aalto log houses that were said to be extant, there does not exist—even at the Alvar Aalto Museum in Jyväskylä—an accurate, publicly available resource documenting the current status of these works (a dramatic contrast to the work of Frank Lloyd Wright, which is vehemently tracked and kept current by such organizations as the Frank Lloyd Wright Foundation). One exception to the rule is Aalto's Villa Vekara in Karstula.

Situated in a remote, densely forested area of Central Finland with only a primitive path connecting it to the nearest road, Villa Vekara is a privately owned summer cabin. It is a peculiar design, in which Nordic Classicism is mixed with

overtly Italian Renaissance–style porch balustrades, quite out of character with the commonly held image of an Aalto design. In the books on Aalto's architecture, the emphasis is placed on his more mature work, most of it done in a softened, nature-embracing Modern idiom. In the majority of buildings from the lesser-known early stages of Aalto's career, however, Nordic Classicism is the dominant idiom. "At the beginning of the 1920s," Aalto historian Markku Lahti points out, "Aalto's architecture was bound up with the times, with the values and ideals prevalent then. The dominant style in Finland was Nordic Classicism."[3]

Simple, attractive, and cozy, Villa Vekara has an eave entry with covered porches off the front and rear and a single-gable roof with unornamented, wide bargeboards and extended eaves to give the logs greater protection from rain and snow. The logs themselves are hewn square in the traditional manner of such noteworthy Karelia-inspired houses as Akseli Gallen-Kallela's Kalela (1889–95) in Ruovesi, Finland, and Pekka Halonen's Halosenniemi (1899–1902) near Helsinki (both of which are open to the public). What is unusual is the way in which the corners are handled: the logs of the walls appear to be tenoned into weight-bearing corner posts. In fact, the corners are notched traditionally but are given false fronts in the form of vertically hung pieces of milled weatherboarding (sometimes called clapboard or simply wooden siding). This suggests there might have been a plan, one that was ultimately aborted, to apply weatherboarding vertically to the entire house in order to achieve what was then regarded as a more refined look. Whether this was done according to Aalto's specification or his client's is unknown, but by the early 1920s the practice of "dressing up" log construction with weatherboarding had become customary in Finland, just as in Sweden and Norway.

A comparison of the finished house (as illustrated here) with the existing drawings suggests that several modifications were made before actual construction commenced. (The drawings that feature these changes must have been lost, as they are absent from the now-published complete catalogue of Aalto's works.) In the version depicted in the drawings, the entry is shown in the gable end, and there is only one

ABOVE This view from the back porch provides a clear perspective of one of several Renaissance-style balustrades and shows how the log walls were joined with a tooth notch and insulated with animal hair.
RIGHT Note that the house depicted in the original drawings differs in a number of ways from the finished building. The drawing at bottom left is the first floor (translation: *Keittiö* = kitchen; *Tuba* = living room/dining room). The second-floor plan shows the master bedroom and a small guest room. The centrally positioned fireplace is designed to heat the entire house.

OPPOSITE As this view of the living room/dining room suggests, Aalto's interior scheme is all about celebrating the natural beauty of the logs. Ornamentation is restricted to the elements of the staircase.

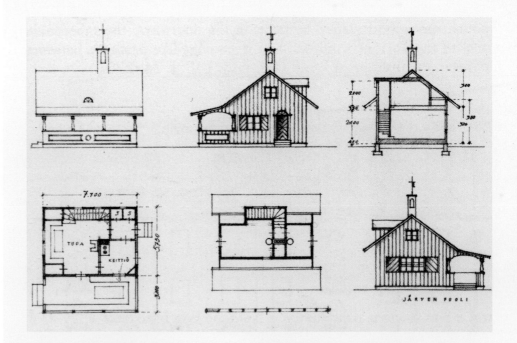

covered porch. The arrangement of the windows is also especially interesting. In the gable end that is shown here, the windows are arranged freely, an "anarchistic" arrangement, as Aalto called it, not in the symmetrical fashion depicted in the drawings. The late Göran Schildt, Aalto's longtime friend and biographer, points out that Aalto began to incorporate this method into his designs after a 1923 study tour of Gunnar Asplund's architecture in Sweden, especially his Villa Snellman (1917), the first building to break away from placing the windows on a vertical axis.[4] It is very likely that Villa Vekara, completed in 1924, had already been in the planning stages before Aalto left on this trip and was revised upon his return from it.

Villa Vekara is a charming example of a small but stylish log cabin, one that would be fitting for use today in practically any forested setting. Schildt described the structure as "an exquisite miniature log cabin, carefully thought out in every detail."[5]

Other log house designs by Aalto worth investigating—each one located in Finland—include the main building (1924) of Alatalo Farm in Tarvaala, the Major Jörgen Schauman Hunting Lodge (1945) in Pertunmaa near Lake Koskionjärvi, the Yhteis-Sisu Oy House (1945) in Vanaja near Hämeenlinna, and Villa Kihlman[6] (1947) on Lake Näsijärvi.

Hellman House

LOCATION
Santa Monica, California

YEAR BUILT
1924

REMODEL ARCHITECT
Alfred Heineman

BUILDER
J. E. Sturgeon

STYLE
Craftsman

There is said to be a scene in the now-lost 1923 silent-movie version of Henry Wadsworth Longfellow's "The Courtship of Miles Standish" in which this log house makes its public debut. At the time, the house had recently been assembled as a stage set for actor, producer, and noted set builder[1] Charles Ray of Charles Ray Productions, and it would have been by necessity a much simpler affair than it is now. The many elaborate, rustic appointments that characterize the interiors of the house today were not put in place until later on, in its second act. That part of the story begins with an ending. Released after eight months of shooting, during which time the production spent the then-exorbitant sum of $800,000, *The Courtship of Miles Standish* turned out to be a classic Hollywood flop.[2]

Before the dust had even settled from the debacle, Ray's bankers, one of whom was Marco Hellman of Hellman Bank in Los Angeles, swooped in and foreclosed on Charles Ray Productions, and he quickly chose to assume ownership of the log house.[3] The process of disassembling and relocating the building from the movie location in Lake Arrowhead, California, to Hellman's new parklike property in the Rustic Canyon enclave of Santa Monica began with the meticulous numbering of each log.[4] The Rustic Canyon property, situated about two miles from the beach at Pacific Palisades, was part of a place called the Uplifters Ranch, a private bohemian social club to which Hellman belonged, along with other prominent Los Angeles businessmen. Many of the club's buildings were done in log construction or log cladding. "The group began holding outings each summer at various resorts and decided after World War I to find a permanent site," notes Rustic Canyon historian Betty Lou Young. "The land in Rustic Canyon was purchased in 1921, a clubhouse built on the floor of the canyon in 1923–24, and summer homes built by the members on two adjacent roads. . . . Most of the homes were rustic in style."[5] Once the pieces of Hellman's new log house had been moved to Rustic Canyon, reconstruction was prompt and many noticeable improvements were made.

Designer Alfred Heineman (1882–1974), who handled the remodeling of Hellman's log house,[6] was the brother of Arthur Heineman of Arthur S. Heineman & Co., one of southern California's most prolific architecture firms during the early twentieth century. From the time Alfred joined his brother's practice, about 1909, until they parted thirty years later, the Heinemans designed some three hundred bungalows, notably the Craftsman-Style landmark Hindry House (1909) and the thirty-six-unit Bowen Court complex (1910–13), both in Pasadena, California.[7] The Heinemans designed many buildings for commercial use as well, including one of the Pig 'n' Whistle restaurants in Los Angeles and a number of Marco Hellman's Los Angeles–area bank buildings. Like that of the architect brothers Charles Greene and Henry Greene of Pasadena, the Heineman brothers' work, though less well known, is among the Craftsman era's most influential.

Although charming in its own way, the exterior view of this former movie stage set is not the main attraction of the house. Unfortunately, we can see in this side elevation that the log work is in need of repair.
The unsightly asphalt shingles were added because the house is located in a fire-prone area; the dormer is also a later addition.

As family businesses often are, Arthur S. Heineman & Co., which for a period had its office in a Marco Hellman–owned building,[8] was a complex arrangement consisting of a controlling, business-savvy individual and a freethinking, creative personality. Historian Robert Winter points out that roles were well defined within the practice, and Alfred, who had studied under designer Ernest Batchelder of Batchelder tile fame, typically served as the lead on creative matters: "Based on an extensive review of their work and our many conversations, it is clear to me that Arthur participated in the first stages of the design process and that Alfred took over after the plan, and perhaps the decorative treatment, had been chosen. He solved the esthetic problems while Arthur, undoubtedly criticizing and finally approving Alfred's drawings, took care of the business and nourished his inventive bent."[9] This helps to explain why the Hellman House remodel is attributed solely to Alfred.

In Heineman's overtly rustic design for the Hellman House interiors, the two most prominent features, both of them in the living room, are elements that echo earlier works by the Heineman firm. The Adirondack-Style balcony that projects into the living room from the second-floor master bedroom derives from the Heinemans' design of the Club House at Bowen Court. The handling of the fireplace in massive boulders is an attribute that can be traced back to the 1909 Hindry House.

Another feature of the interior, one that is not a Heineman trademark, speaks of the revelry the house was famous for in the heyday of the Uplifters Club. During Prohibition, Hellman installed in the wooden-slab countertop of the bar, which is located just beyond the living room, a pump that allowed beer to be drawn from a container stored safely out of sight in the basement. The pump is still there today.

The Hellman House remained in Hellman's possession until the end of the Great Depression, during which time he, like many other Uplifters, saw his fortune dwindle to nothing. Joseph Musgrove, a lawyer for the Uplifters Club, fared better; he took over ownership of the log house from Hellman and kept it until 1966. He periodically rented the house to California's Governor Earl Warren, who used it as a getaway for himself and his family. Subsequent owners modernized and enlarged the kitchen, which faces the back of the property, and installed skylights in the living room.

The current owner bought the Hellman House from actress Daryl Hannah and has painstakingly sought out and reinstalled a number of the house's original custom-made rustic furnishings that were removed by various owners over the years. Currently awaiting Historic Cultural Monument status from the City of Los Angeles, the log house is his primary home.

ABOVE The massive cobblestone-and-boulder chimney, perhaps the most picturesque feature of the exterior, is 16 feet wide at its base. The front of the house is at the far left in the photograph.

OPPOSITE, TOP The property slopes steeply downward to the right of the driveway in front of the house, making it impossible to photograph the façade head-on. Notice the grille on the gable window. This part of the house has been essentially untouched since the 1920s.

BOTTOM Like most exterior building materials, logs require periodic upkeep, and parts of the Hellman House need such attention and care, as this wall detail suggests.

RIGHT This sketch of the living room was found in Alfred Heineman's archives. Compare it with the finished product, shown on the opposite page.

BELOW, LEFT The interiors of the 2,300-square-foot house are rich in fascinating rustic design details, such as these hand-forged and -hammered iron strap hinges on the heavily distressed wide plank Dutch door.

BELOW, RIGHT This end of the living room (to the right of the door depicted in the drawing) has French doors that open onto the patio shown on page 92. The interiors have been rechinked in recent years.

OPPOSITE An Adirondack-style balcony, whose posts and limbs are made of eucalyptus, projects from the second-floor master bedroom, about 8½ feet above the floor of the living room. The positioning of the balcony directly in front of the fireplace has to be intentional. The custom-made hand-forged wrought-iron chandeliers hanging from the 14-foot ceiling depict members of the Hellman family with their horses. On the left side of the balcony is an additional bedroom, which is now used as the cigar lounge, and on the opposite side is the stair to the second floor and a hallway that leads to the kitchen and the first-floor bathroom. In most areas of the house, the original bark of the logs remains intact.

ABOVE The idea of rustic design is beautifully
articulated in the living room, where a 10-foot-wide
cobblestone-and-boulder fireplace is the central
focus. The four skylights are a recent addition, the only
substantial alterations to this part of the house.

OPPOSITE Hellman House's sublime rusticity is
at its most pronounced at the stair that leads to the
master bedroom, bathroom, and guest bedroom.
Another bathroom is located at the end of the hallway,
on the right, just past the entrance to the kitchen.

The Point

(formerly Camp Wonundra)

LOCATION
Upper Saranac Lake, New York

YEAR BUILT
1930–33

ARCHITECT
William G. Distin

STYLE
Adirondack

ABOVE Distin's pencil sketch, prepared for William A. Rockefeller, depicts the rear elevation of the camp's main building. Note the various sporting activities that are illustrated in the corners.

OPPOSITE From the expansive deck, which overlooks Saranac Lake, one can see that bay windows dominate the house's rear elevation. Compare this composition to the original drawing by Distin. The bargeboards are new, part of a recent roof restoration.

In 1930, fifty-four years after developer and self-trained designer William West Durant first arrived in the rugged Adirondack wilderness of upper New York State, where he subsequently formalized a rustic vernacular that would eventually find widespread national application as the Adirondack style, a selection of pine logs was being marked for the construction of yet another camp in the Durant tradition. By and large, the erection of a new camp was a relatively unusual event at this time. The boundless spending in the region by America's leading financiers, railroad magnates, and industrialists that had produced such architectural monuments of the style as Durant's Camp Pine Knot (1877) and Sagamore Lodge (1896) was long over. By the time of the stock-market crash in 1929, the local timber supply had been depleted, so that those who sought to make a substantial repair or to expand an existing camp property had to haul in logs from Canada. Still, despite the challenging times, one young man, at the age of thirty-four, had grand plans for a site in the Adirondacks, and his means more than equaled his ambitions.

New York's Adirondack Mountain region has a greater concentration of log architecture, much of it architect-designed, than any other place in the United States. It is also the area where the concept of the Great Camp originated. National Park Service historian Linda Flint McClelland explains:

> The great camps of New York's Adirondack region provided one of the earliest and strongest expressions of [Andrew Jackson] Downing's ideas for a picturesque rustic style appropriate for a natural area or wilderness. Nestled at the edge of deep forests, the camps were frequently lakeside resorts consisting of several buildings separated by function. As it evolved in the late nineteenth century, the Adirondack style adopted features of the Shingle Style, the local vernacular of pioneer log cabins, and the romantic European styles of country homes, especially the chalet form of the Swiss Alps and the German farmhouse with jerkinhead [a shape intermediate between a gable and a hip] gables.[1]

Although the Rockefellers at one point owned more than 85,000 acres in the Adirondacks,[2] Camp Wonundra, commissioned by William Avery Rockefeller (1896–1973), is the only Great Camp built by a member of the family. Sited on a seventy-five-acre peninsula at Whitney Point in Upper Saranac Lake, Camp Wonundra consists of nine independent buildings—each a frame structure with log-slab cladding. The primary building, the lodge, is a single-story arrangement in a butterfly-plan shape. Its domestic scale and effective dispersion of public and private spaces in separate wings—in all, three bedrooms, library, dining room, great hall, kitchen/service area, and baths—make it, perhaps more than any other extant Great Camp, especially worthy of study for anyone now looking to build a single-family house in the Adirondack style.

Camp Wonundra was created by one of the region's veteran architects, William G. Distin (1884–1970). "It is said that Distin first conceived of it as his own dream house, but could never afford to build it," observes journalist Eliza Scott Harris. "One day Rockefeller, a recluse who liked to fish and enjoyed his drink, saw the plans on Distin's desk and said, 'I want you to build that for me.'"[3]

Distin had deep roots in the Adirondacks. After graduating from Saranac Lake High School in 1900, he went to work for architect William Coulter (ca. 1864–1907), whose design office in Saranac Lake was one of the busiest in the Adirondacks. Coulter, who is responsible for the designs of such multi-building log complexes as Pinebrook (ca. 1898), Knollwood Club (ca. 1900), and Sagamore Lodge's Amusement Hall (ca. 1901), had moved his practice from New York City to the Adirondacks in 1897 and quickly found his footing working in the popular rustic tradition established by Durant. As historian Harvey H. Kaiser points out, "Coulter was an admirer of Durant, and his designs followed Durant's influence."[4]

After Coulter died in 1907, Distin attended New York's Columbia University, where he earned a degree in architecture in 1910. Craig Gilborn, former director of the Adirondack Museum, suggests that in 1912 or 1913 Distin rejoined Coulter's practice, which was then run by architect Max Westhoff, and was eventually made partner.[5] Except for a year of war-effort work in Washington, D.C., in 1917–18, Distin stayed in Saranac Lake and continued the Coulter office's tradition of working primarily in log construction in the Durant mode, mostly for wealthy clients. Kaiser recalls Distin's particular skill with handling the most demanding of these clients: "It was Will Distin who was told by one New York client, after approval of a camp design, 'I'm leaving for Europe. I want it built and finished the day I return.' As the camp neared completion, the owner cabled, 'Will arrive Thursday. Please buy dishes, and have roast lamb for dinner.' The owner arrived, and as the story goes, china, silver, flowers, and roast lamb were on the table."[6]

Although the Great Camp era was gradually coming to an end by the time Distin designed Camp Wonundra,[7] he had already left an indelible mark on the area. Before his work for Rockefeller, Distin completed about twenty camps and cottages in the Adirondacks,[8] many of them at Upper Saranac Lake, including portions of the twenty-eight-structure Lewisohn Camp (1903–30) at Prospect Point, the camp at Indian Point (ca. 1928), and the camp at Markham Point (ca. 1929).

Rockefeller kept Camp Wonundra under his care throughout much of his lifetime, finally selling it in 1969 to an individual who turned it into a family getaway. By 1978 Camp Wonundra's ownership had transferred again, this time to fine-art photographer and noted travel writer Robert Carter. Carter eventually renamed the property The Point and turned it into an award-winning hotel. In 1986 he sold it to the present owner, Garrett Hotel Group, under whose management the eleven-room hotel has continually been ranked among the best in the world.

ABOVE Distin and Rockefeller opted for Canadian pine logs, each with an average diameter of 20 inches. In keeping with the Adirondack Style tradition established by early developer-designer William West Durant in the late 1870s, notably in the buildings of Camp Pine Knot, the log ends are left round. A wool-like material is used as insulation between each log.

OPPOSITE The front elevation of the main building, viewed from the entrance to the property. Distin's highly effective plan places the great hall—the primary gathering place—at the center of a multi-winged configuration.

ABOVE Adirondack historian Craig Gilborn points out that the octagonal entry hall, here fronted by Dutch door, is a Distin trademark.

OPPOSITE The great hall is 40 feet wide by 26 feet deep with massive 10-foot-wide fireplaces, one at each end of the room. One's eye is immediately drawn to the ceiling's king-post trusses—each with elaborate wrought-iron strap braces. To the left of the old piano is the octagonal entry hall.

ABOVE A view of the octagonal entry hall from just inside the front door

OPPOSITE, TOP The library's interiors epitomize the notion of rustic elegance.
BOTTOM The bathroom of the library, like the others in the house, has been tastefully modernized.

Helburn House

LOCATION
Bozeman, Montana

YEAR BUILT
1951

ARCHITECT
Richard Neutra

STYLE
Modern

For an architect whose body of work has been thoroughly analyzed as the subject of more than a dozen books and museum exhibits, and hundreds of magazine and journal articles, it is astonishing how Modern master Richard Neutra's most peculiar residential design—his only log house—has thus far existed largely off the radar of critical attention. Its only real exposure came in October 2002 at the Chicago Architecture Foundation's ArchiCenter exhibition "Neutra in Montana: The Blurring of Architecture and Landscape." Even Neutra's longtime collaborator, photographer Julius Shulman, had never heard of it: "What? A log house?" he exclaimed with utter surprise. "Well, he must've done it tongue in cheek!"[1]

Shulman's almost apologetic response to learning of Neutra's venture into an area of practice that many Modernists regard as negligible helps to explain why the Helburn House is one work that is not described visually or textually in any of the books on Neutra. Even the recent landmark book *Richard Neutra: The Complete Works* (2003) acknowledges the Helburn House only to the extent of specifying its title and chronological position in the oeuvre. For the popular notion of rusticity, which by common definition implies a certain lack of sophistication, is, after all, at odds with the popularly held idea of Modern. Modernists aren't supposed to like or even be interested in rustic architecture. For them the very idea of Modern architecture is based on an appropriation of the latest technological advancements in building concepts and materials, so a Modern house bearing overtly rustic features is an anomaly; it doesn't fit the mold. Or does it?

The Vienna-born Neutra (1892–1970) is best known for his pioneering use of cutting-edge technologies and new materials in industrial-minded works such as the Lovell Health House (1929) in Los Angeles, the first International Style house in the United States and the project that first brought Neutra international acclaim, and the Kaufman House (1946) in the desert of Palm Springs, California. Nonetheless, at the request of certain clients,[2] Neutra had begun to produce designs in a softened, woodsy Modern idiom—a populist's Modernism—long before he designed this home for the Helburn family. One such example is the Darling House (1937) in San Francisco, which he and then partner Otto Winkler sheathed from top to bottom in one-by-six-foot redwood boards. It was the first in a line of houses that were unquestionably Modern but possessed certain attributes that could be called rustic—characteristics that, in addition to imparting a sense of warmth, furthered Neutra's overriding agenda of seamlessly integrating structure with nature.

In Monterey, California, in 1939 Neutra completed the Davey House with its redwood tongue-and-groove siding. In 1941 his design for the acclaimed Nesbitt House in Los Angeles, included, in addition to an array of Neutraesque Modern features, a woodsy interior distinguished by wood-paneled walls, multiple custom built-ins done in naturally finished redwood plywood, and a floor of brick below a

The front elevation, seen from the bottom of the front yard. The roof overhang extends 7 feet beyond the walls of the house.

ceiling marked by exposed redwood beams. The exterior was clad in weeping brick in concert with rough-sawn board and batten,[3] which he discussed in his description of the Nesbitt House in *Richard Neutra on Building: Mystery and Realities of the Site* (1951): "The rough-sawn lumber and the rough mortar lines repeat Nature's textures."[4]

Both the weeping brick and board-and-batten schemes had by the late 1930s become staples of the inherently rustic ranch house designs of Californian Cliff May (1908–1989) and others—an approach to building that would soon become an American cultural phenomenon. Each of the "woodsy" Neutra houses belongs to a group of designs that can be classified as being at once Modern and to a degree rustic, at least as rustic as numerous ranch-house designs of the same period. Moreover, in this way, these Neutra works presaged the use of logs at Helburn House.

In February 1947, *Time* magazine ran a feature story called "Homes Inside Out" about Richard Neutra's nature-embracing work. "He will travel anywhere to make sure his buildings fit the landscape, the people, and the weather," the writer noted. Neutra was then one of the most sought-after architects in the United States, with a reputation "second only to lordly Frank Lloyd Wright."[5] Two decades earlier, during

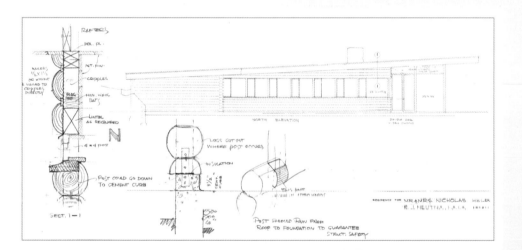

a four-month stretch from late 1924 to early 1925, Neutra had worked as a draftsman in Wright's office at Taliesin in Spring Green, Wisconsin, although for various reasons, both personal and professional, the arrangement did not last long. Neutra soon succumbed to the persuasive powers of his Viennese friend and former schoolmate (and fellow disciple of Adolf Loos) R. M. Schindler and traded chilly Wisconsin for sunny southern California. As it was for Wright in the works he completed there, the climate of southern California was especially conducive to Neutra's progressive ideas about opening up the house to nature. Having temporarily occupied the guest wing of Schindler's new concrete-and-redwood home in Hollywood, Neutra began in earnest the work that would result over the next two decades in his well-documented ascendancy to the top of his field.

During this period of Neutra's career, 1949 was a decisive year, for things had come to a head on multiple fronts. In certain ways it was the end of one important era and the beginning of a very different one. "Indeed, Neutra's period of personal creativity," writes his biographer Thomas S. Hines, "had been the years between 1927 and 1949, during which time he was without doubt the leading modernist residential designer."[6] Neutra suffered a heart attack in 1949—perhaps the only kind of event that could have forced the notoriously workaholic architect to slow down. Another life-altering event of the year was his second *Time* feature story, which appeared on August 15. This time Neutra was pictured on the cover of the enor-

ABOVE Neutra provided construction-detail drawings that show exactly how he wanted the logs to be handled. The drawing identified as "North Elevation" depicts an early version of the back of the house.

OPPOSITE The 2,500-square-foot house is built into the site's natural slope, which tumbles down toward Sourdough Creek. Little more than the gently pitched flat sod roof can be seen from the nearby road. Inside the row of windows next to the front door is a large built-in planter, a common feature in Neutra houses.

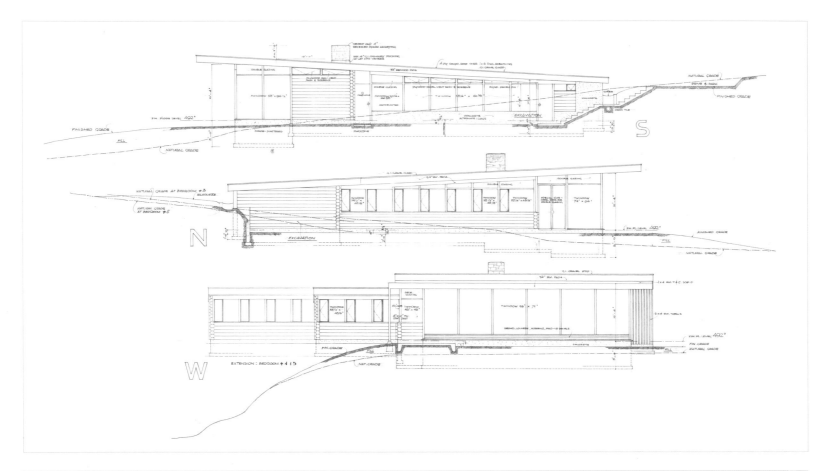

OPPOSITE, TOP The south-, north-, and west-facing elevations, respectively, as prepared by Neutra's residential practice. The top drawing is the front of the house; note the foundation level in relation to the line of the natural grade. These drawings ultimately received certain alterations.

BOTTOM As one would expect of a Neutra design, the Helburn House uses glass walls in order to visually unify indoor and outdoor space. Each glass panel on this side is 72 inches wide and 94 inches high.

mously popular, internationally distributed magazine, and for the next few years, Neutra was in high demand even in remote parts of the United States.[7]

Of greatest relevance to the focus of the present book, however, is another event that took place in the summer of 1949: Montana State University's (MSU) invitation to Neutra to deliver a lecture at the school's main campus in Bozeman on the subject of urbanism in the American West. As he had done so often with similar requests from organizations all over the world, Neutra agreed to the visit and welcomed the opportunity to spread his message. Present that day in the campus auditorium where Neutra gave his talk was MSU professor of geography Nicholas Helburn, who found Neutra to be particularly impressive—enough to compel the young professor to commission Neutra to design a house for himself and his wife.[8]

In September 1950, after producing multiple preliminary studies and a number of alterations to the original design, the final floor plan for the three-bedroom, two-and-a-half-bath "Residence of Dr. and Mrs. Nicholas Helburn" was issued by Neutra's Silverlake Boulevard office. As the drawings themselves reveal, Neutra provided detailed instructions to the contractor, a Bozeman firm, on how to integrate the log cladding with his post-and-beam structural framework, as well as provisions for the eventual addition of two more bedrooms.

Some of Neutra's instructions were not followed. The spiderleg outrigger,[9] a feature that had become a signature statement in Neutra's career, is part of the plan but was left out of the house's construction. After reviewing photographs of the finished house, Dion Neutra (1926–), Richard's architect son, longtime creative collaborator and business partner, and principal of Richard and Dion Neutra Architects in Los Angeles, suggested that some significant interior and exterior finish details had been handled in a manner that the Neutra office would not have approved.[10] Examples include "the use of logs as lintels and posts in lieu of the usual Neutra detailing for the windows, as well as more of the exterior wall panels executed with logs."

According to Montana State University architecture professor John Brittingham, the use of logs is one aspect of the design that was always part of the plan: "From Nick Helburn's recounting of the history of the project, it is clear that he and Neutra decided the house was to be of log construction from the outset and that this decision was made with financial, technical, and aesthetic concerns in mind. Neutra's office articulated that it would work in collaboration with local builders' practices in log construction."[11]

Despite the fact that it now needs extensive restoration, the Helburn House, one of only two Neutra houses in Montana, is well worth preserving. It is one of the finest living demonstrations of how, during the mid-century Modern period, warm, rustic materials were merged with the typically cool Modern-era aesthetic to create a thoroughly harmonious living space.

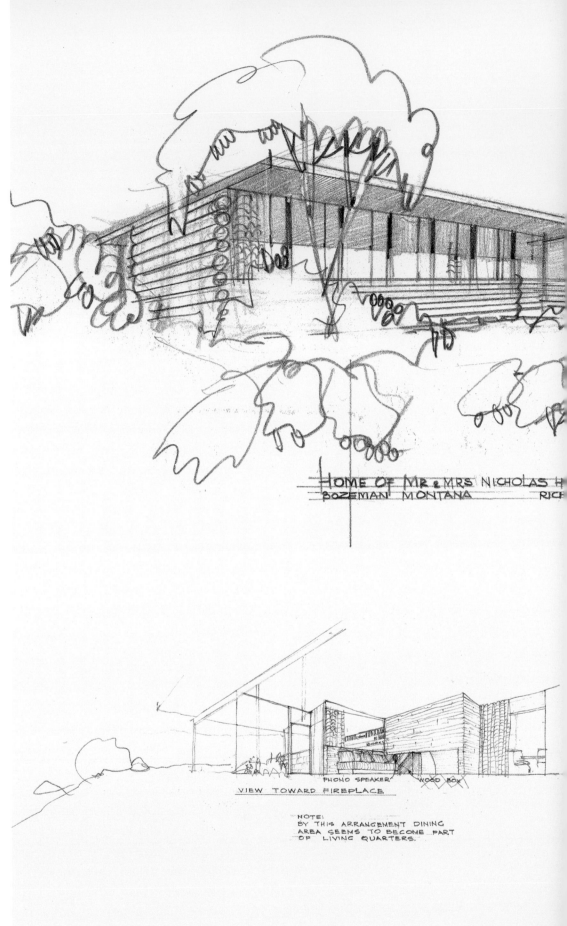

HOME OF MR & MRS NICHOLAS H
BOZEMAN MONTANA   RICH

VIEW TOWARD FIREPLACE

PHONO SPEAKER   WOOD BOX

NOTE:
BY THIS ARRANGEMENT DINING
AREA SEEMS TO BECOME PART
OF LIVING QUARTERS.

TOP Neutra's perspective drawings are always elegant. The dates on this and other drawings in the Helburn file of the Neutra archive at UCLA suggest that this was one of the first drawings he did for the project, probably executed before he saw the site. Even at this early stage, log construction was part of the design. Note the presence of the spider-leg outrigger (the arm projecting into the landscape from beneath the roof overhang), a signature Neutra structural feature that for some reason was not used in the actual construction.

BOTTOM, LEFT The living room is the heart of this house. The built-in settee next to the broad hearth is another signature Neutra feature. He also specified custom built-in cabinetry for audio equipment, which is still in surprisingly good condition. However, the log theme is not carried through to the interior, here or elsewhere in the house. Instead, the walls are done simply in Sheetrock, the windows framed richly in milled Philippine mahogany. The massive fireplace, which is positioned between the living room and the open dining room, is clad in fieldstone, but at some point during the house's three changes of ownership, unfortunately, the stone was given a coat of red latex paint.

BOTTOM, RIGHT This floor plan, one of many in the archive, was the latest issued by Neutra's office. Note the inclusion of a "future extension" at the northernmost end, along with the presence of a 4-by-4-inch post (part of the spider-leg outrigger) positioned off the area labeled "terrace."

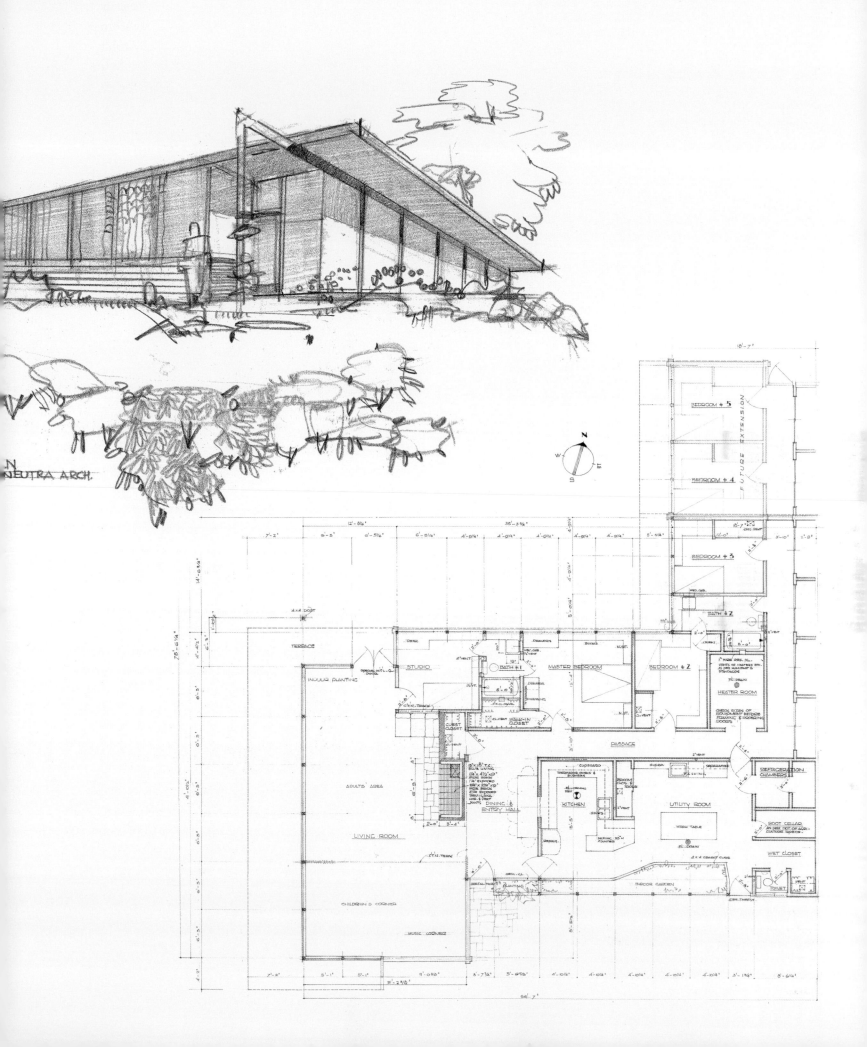

NEUTRA ARCH.

Le Petit Cabanon

LOCATION
Roquebrune-Cap-Martin, France

YEAR BUILT
1952

ARCHITECT
Le Corbusier

BUILDER
Charles Barberis

STYLE
Modern

It is hard to imagine a more romantic one-room getaway than Le Corbusier's cabin by the sea. This is the first complete view of the structure that one has after negotiating the steps down the side of the cliff from the path that runs above the house. Notice that Corbusier has caused the building to hover over the ground (four inches to be precise) by resting each corner on blocks of stone. For decades after Le Corbusier's death in 1965, scholars of his work ignored or overlooked this building.

On December 30, 1951, the world-renowned Modernist architect and designer Le Corbusier (1887–1965) was seated in the quaint café L'Etoile de Mer in the sleepy resort town of Roquebrune-Cap-Martin, France, where he had vacationed nearly every year since the late 1920s. He had recently completed his contribution to the development of the United Nations headquarters building in New York City, and his Chapel of Notre Dame-du-Haut in Ronchamp and the city plan and an array of governmental buildings for Chandigarh in India were among his ongoing projects. Although much of Roquebrune-Cap-Martin had succumbed to overdevelopment decades earlier, this particular edge of the city, which sits on the shore of the Mediterranean, still retained an air of seclusion and tranquility (as it does even today). During the many years he visited the town, Le Corbusier was usually the guest of his longtime friends Jean Badovici, editor of *L'Architecture Vivante*, and the designer Eileen Gray. In 1926–29 Badovici and Gray had built themselves after Gray's design a very modern house, which they called E.1027, located just down the hill from where the café was later built. "He often returned to E.1027, especially after the war, driving his tiny apple-green Fiat up the hill to spend a few days with Badovici," wrote Gray's biographer, Peter Adam.[1]

On this particular day in December 1951, Le Corbusier had come not to see Badovici but to put his ideas on paper for a house of his own to be built here—the only house he ever designed for himself, a birthday gift for his wife, Yvonne. A year earlier, he had worked out a deal with the owner of the café, Thomas Rebutato, to acquire a small plot right next to the restaurant.[2] Because of a falling out with Badovici and Gray, it was necessary for Le Corbusier to establish a place of his own if he wished to continue vacationing in this exclusive part of Roquebrune, where land was very scarce. The dispute had begun in 1938, when Le Corbusier painted a series of sexually oriented murals on some walls of E.1027 without their permission, and it heated up again in 1948, when he published photographs of the murals in the magazine *L'Architecture d'Aujourd'hui* without crediting the house to Badovici and Gray.[3]

The timing of Le Corbusier's visit to Roquebrune that December and the subsequent fast-paced construction of his house was to a significant degree determined by his wife's failing health. She had by 1951 become very ill with chronic gastritis and osteoporosis. As historians Sarah Menin and Flora Samuel suggest, Le Corbusier had long regarded this particular spot in the Côte d'Azur as especially conducive to healing and was thus the only place for his wife to be: it was "essential to understand that Le Corbusier felt that the mystical richness of the setting was the greatest medicine he could provide."[4]

According to legend,[5] while he was sitting in the café that day, Le Corbusier spent a total of forty-five minutes designing the cabin. Its plan was based on Le Modulor,

OPPOSITE From inside the cabin one can see Pointe de la Vieille in the distance. When the sun is shining, this part of the Mediterranean Sea turns a beautiful shade of turquoise.

BELOW When a log is plain sawn, the first lengthwise cut results in an outer slab, typically the least valuable part of the log. The outer walls of the frame structure are completely clad in these cast-off pine log slabs, each about two inches thick. Builder Charles Barberis treated them like milled clapboards; each piece overlaps the other so that rain will run off the wall surfaces. Given the indiscriminate use of the nails, it seems clear that fine craftsmanship was not an issue in this aspect of the construction.

a scale of proportions devised by Le Corbusier on the basis of the Golden Section and said to be in complete harmony with human measurements and thus health-inducing. Not to be confused with modular construction, the concept of Le Modulor had first been brought to Le Corbusier's attention in 1946 by Albert Einstein, who claimed that it "makes the bad difficult and the good easy."[6] As historian Bruno Chiambretto explains in the book Le Corbusier à Cap-Martin, the Modulor is made manifest in the cabin by dividing the overall volume of 366 cm × 366 cm into four equal rectangles spiraling around a central square of 86 cm.[7] Since each rectangle contains a separate function, the cabin interior is the epitome of spatial efficiency and, in spite of its small size, feels both inviting and comfortable. Each of its strategically placed windows frames a carefully considered view of the landscape and sea.

Although it can accurately be said that in his typical fashion Le Corbusier rigorously addressed every last detail of the cabin's architecture and furniture, certain other details went unattended. For one, it has been well documented that Yvonne, who had difficulty walking (she died in 1957), had to be carried up and down the unreasonably steep path to the cabin in a wheelbarrow.

Le Corbusier's decision to clad a prefabricated, standard frame structure of milled studding in pine-log slabs is the most unusual aspect of the cabin and the feature that has come to define it, particularly among the many international tourists who visit it each year. Architect and author Kenneth Frampton has pointed out that the use of log cladding was a last-minute decision; Le Corbusier had never before used a rustic building material so prominently in his architecture.

Le Corbusier lived in Le Petit Cabanon until his death in 1965, when he suffered a heart attack while swimming in the ocean in front of the property. Interestingly, he had once told the famous photographer Brassaï, "I feel so good in my *cabanon* that without a doubt I will meet my end here."

In 2005, when the photographer and I arrived at the cabin, now a government-protected landmark, a very knowledgeable representative from the municipality of Roquebrune led us on the tour and explained that the site had recently become very popular. Only a few weeks earlier, she had guided actor and architecture buff Brad Pitt through the house. Beaming, she explained that Pitt had carefully inspected and photographed Le Corbusier's entire property and seemed very excited to be there.

RIGHT In light of the greatness of Le Corbusier's buildings for other people, it is fascinating to see how he handled details such as this in his own house. Note that the slabs are pine and that the windows are framed in oak.

BELOW This is one of the more beautiful vantage points from which to see the house, and it also enables us to see how the architect pitched the flat roof in order to give the south-facing front elevation more sunlight. The front of the house rises to just under 11 feet, whereas the back reaches a height of just over 9 feet. The span of this log wall is 12 feet, 8 inches.

TOP When the front door slides open to the side (note the copper hardware of the lock), the narrow entry hall (23¾ in. wide) comes into focus. Everything is original here, including the murals by Le Corbusier. On the wall at the far end of the hall is a closet, which has an array of knobs that serve as a coat rack.

BOTTOM The floorplan key:

1. front entry
2. secret passage to the bar of Étoile de Mer café
3. closet
4. end of entry hall
5. bathroom
6. built-in wardrobe cabinet
7. single bed (originally 1 of 2) with built-in storage compartments underneath
8. low table (now positioned where bed 2 used to be)
9. single bed (removed after the death of Le Corbusier's wife)
10. storage cabinet and sink
11. dining table with a box stool on each side
12. low shelf
13. shelf
14. vertically oriented window
15. rectangular window (27¾ in. tall by 25½ in. wide)
16. horizontal window (13 in. tall by 28 in. wide)

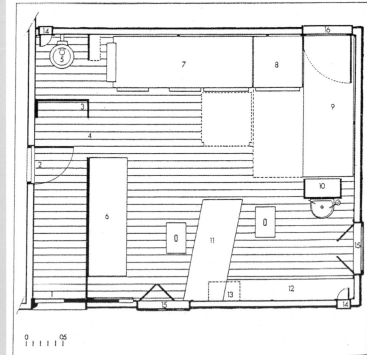

OPPOSITE After passing through the entry hall (the hallway murals are at the right in the background of this photograph), one arrives in this space. The walls are clad in quarter-inch plywood (probably birch), the seams of which are covered with a thin strip of molding. For the purpose of overhead storage, Le Corbusier gave part of the cabin a drop ceiling clad with fiberboard panels. Although the evidence is inconclusive, there is reason to believe that the wardrobe cabinet, walnut dining table, and other built-ins were designed by Charlotte Perriand or Jean Prouvé, each of whom was working with Le Corbusier at the time.

ABOVE, LEFT This corner is situated opposite the dining table, which sits where an additional bed was originally placed. The four-inch-wide floorboards are chestnut.

ABOVE, RIGHT Above the walnut dining table, the most lavish piece of furniture in the cabin, we see the sink and storage-cabinet—what Le Corbusier called the "sanitary column." The wall sconce above the window, like the others shown in these photographs, is original.

RIGHT The oddest decision made by Le Corbusier in this house is his positioning of the bed next to the toilet, where only a curtain stands between the toilet bowl and the built-in headrest. This perspective also shows the built-in drawers of the bed. To give one an idea of how compact a space this is, consider that the closet of the entry hall (notice the protruding knobs of the coat rack) is immediately to the left of the toilet space.

Pearlman Cabin

LOCATION
Idyllwild, California

YEAR BUILT
1957

ARCHITECT
John Lautner

BUILDER
William Branch

STYLE
Organic

John Lautner was known for his exotic house designs, in particular the Chemosphere House in Los Angeles, but it is only after one learns about his lifelong relationship with his family's traditional log house that this flying saucer docked on logs begins to make sense.

For the mountainside property in Idyllwild, California, that belonged to herself and her husband, Agnes Pearlman sought an architect who could give her family of four a progressively designed but small, inexpensive vacation cabin. The year was 1956, and Pearlman, a resident of Los Angeles, was having trouble finding an architect who would take the job. "Mom didn't want an ordinary four-walled log cabin," recalls Pearlman's daughter (and present owner of the house), Nancy Pearlman. "That's what they were building up here then."[1] The site had its challenges, too. Difficult to access through the area's steep, narrow, and rocky unpaved roads, the property was situated on a boulder-strewn slope and had an enormous rock outcropping in the very spot where a house would have optimal views of the adjacent mountain range.

Finally, one of the architects who turned down the job suggested that Pearlman see the Los Angeles–based John Lautner (1911–1994), a Frank Lloyd Wright protégé who had by this time completed a number of his own houses. All of these projects were regarded as very progressive designs, some of which—the Polin and Jacobsen Houses (1949) and the Baldwin House (1955)—featured highly inventive solutions for their steep sites in the hills of Los Angeles. Pearlman, a piano player, soon met Lautner, a devoted admirer of jazz legend Duke Ellington,[2] and the process of creating the highly unusual Pearlman Cabin began. As Nancy Pearlman remembers, "Mom had studied interior design and Modern architecture in the 1940s. She knew Lautner had worked for Frank Lloyd Wright, and she liked Wright's work because his houses fit into the landscape."

Directly after high school, in 1933, Lautner spent five years working for Wright as an apprentice in his Taliesin Fellowship, a unique live-in educational program for aspiring architects that Wright and his third wife, Olgivanna, had launched in 1932 from Taliesin, in Spring Green, Wisconsin. This was a learning-by-doing process for Lautner, and it eventually included direct involvement, as either a draftsman or a project superintendent, in a number of Wright's biggest projects at the time. These included the Roberts House (1937) in Marquette, Michigan (a house commissioned by Lautner's mother-in-law); the house known as Wingspread (1937) in Wind Point, Wisconsin; and the complex of residence/workshop buildings called Taliesin West (1937) in Scottsdale, Arizona.

Lautner remained part of the Taliesin Fellowship until 1938, when he left to establish his own architectural practice in Los Angeles. He would eventually become one of the only apprentices to break free, to expand the basic principles of Wright's "organic architecture" to the point of establishing his own distinct language of design. Because he designed mostly private homes, however, Lautner's genius went largely unrecognized during his lifetime. It has only been in recent years, since the publication of a number of books on his oeuvre, that his work has received wide-

spread acknowledgment for its importance to twentieth-century architecture.

As it turned out, Agnes Pearlman's architect, one of the most progressive designers of houses in the United States at the time, was also intimately acquainted with traditional log-cabin design and construction—the very kind of house that Pearlman did not want for the family's property in Idyllwild.

Lautner, at the age of twelve, had helped his father build the family's summer house in Michigan on Lake Superior. Constructed after a design by Lautner's mother, inspired by the typical Swiss Chalet type, the all-log Lautner house (ca. 1923; see page 20) was the architect's first exposure to this type of building. He owned the house all his life, routinely going there for vacations from his home in Los Angeles. "He always had very fond memories of the log cabin," says Helen Arahuete, Lautner's former chief architect and now a principal of Lautner Associates Architects in Los Angeles. "That experience marked him."[3]

Although there is no evidence that the Lautner house on Lake Superior had any bearing on his decision to use logs prominently in his design for the Pearlman Cabin (Lautner's career-long core design principle of creating a one-of-a-kind solution for each individual site repudiates this supposition outright), it could have served him as an example of what not to do on certain design levels. In the context of his only house design to feature logs, it is intriguing to consider the possibilities that arise from Lautner's having had a lifelong relationship with a traditional log house.[4]

Indeed, Lautner's design for the Pearlman Cabin has little if anything in common with his family's log house or with any other house featured in this book. The Pearlman Cabin is included here simply because the effectiveness of its design is dependent on the use of logs. Throughout his sixty-year career, Lautner frequently reinvented the notion of the house (one example is the 1961 Chemosphere House in Los Angeles), and so often completely dumbfounded onlookers that this author has no qualms about referring to the Pearlman building, which looks like a flying saucer set on logs, as a "log cabin."

Although the design of the Pearlman Cabin, especially in the context of this book, may border on the radical, its warming effect on those who use the house is much like that of more traditional log-house designs. As Nancy Pearlman enthusiastically pointed out during our visit to the house: "You sit here [in the circular main room] and work, and you feel as though you're in the forest, even though you're inside!"

The Lautner family log house was designed by his mother and built by his father about 1923 on the shore of Michigan's Lake Superior. Lautner was intimately acquainted with its construction; indeed, he retained ownership of the house until his death. Note the overhanging second story and the corbelled logs, details that are evident on some of the buildings shown in the "Some Prototypes" chapter in this book. Lautner likely took this photograph of restoration work-in-progress.

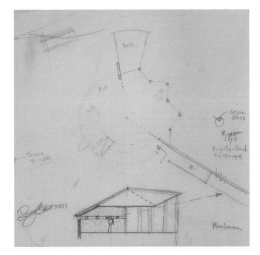

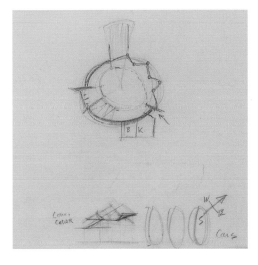

LEFT, TOP This original drawing by Lautner shows, among other details, how he planned to fit glass into the vertical logs.

LEFT, BOTTOM This preliminary sketch leaves out the wing that contains the bathroom and bedroom.

RIGHT From the living room deck, one can see how the ceiling is angled upward for better views of the nearby mountain peak. Lautner positioned the logs in a staggered arrangement in order to angle the glass and minimize glare and reflection, a solution that approximates the work of Mother Nature more closely than a straight line would have done. The small bedroom wing is in the background.

ABOVE Precisely cut grooves were made in each log so the sheets of glass could be neatly inserted.

RIGHT, TOP The circular plan places the house's various functions and features—kitchen, built-in beds, and fireplace—on the outer edge of the centrally positioned dining area. The counter and the built-in shelves next to it define the kitchen area. To the right of the shelving is one of two beds that follow the curve of the wall.

RIGHT, BOTTOM This part of the circular room, if not the entire house, was designed for pulling up a chair and taking time out to appreciate nature and listening to music. The logs that serve as mullions between each "window" create the effect of trees growing through the house. Some would argue that such a panorama eliminates the need for works of art on the walls.

OPPOSITE, TOP LEFT The foundation, like the rest of the building, has endured the past half century without requiring much in the way of upkeep. The original construction was not so easy, however. Owner Nancy Pearlman remembers this well: "They couldn't get anybody up here to build it according to Lautner's design. My uncle, who built the house with my mother's help, lived here on the property in a tent while he was constructing it."

TOP RIGHT This doorway at the front of the house opens to a space behind the living room, next to the beds. The desk was designed for the house by Nancy Pearlman's mother, Agnes. The poured-concrete walls seen here wrap around to meet the wall of glass.

BOTTOM The door from the living room to the deck is at the right in this photograph.

Terry House

LOCATION
Lopez Island, Washington

YEAR BUILT
1959–63

ARCHITECT
Roland Terry

STYLE
Pacific Northwest Modern

A flagstone path begins in a small clearing in the densely forested front end of the property and eventually leads one past the studio building and the reflecting pool and onto this moss-covered rock outcropping, which overlooks the house and the sound. The architecture doesn't compete with the natural setting but appears to be part of it.

It is not surprising that the center of America's timber industry, the Pacific Northwest region of Oregon and Washington, is the location of a broad stylistic range of inventively designed log homes, from the historic to the contemporary. None of them, however, matches the singular beauty of architect Roland Terry's own house on Washington's breathtaking Lopez Island. Built at the edge of a cliff overlooking Puget Sound with massive cedar driftwood logs that were gathered for the project from the Puget's shores, the Terry House is a nonconformist's log house. Instead of being horizontally laid and joined at the corners to form the walls of the building, as in conventional log-house construction, these logs are vertically oriented and used as structural posts. Besides forming the basis of the structure, the house's fifteen logs, at an average diameter of eighty-seven inches, are what make the design an aesthetic success.

Along with Oregon's John Yeon (1910–1994), whose Watzek House (1937) in Portland marks the unofficial beginning of the style, Seattle architect Roland Terry (born 1917) is a pioneer of Pacific Northwest Modern-style architecture. Throughout the 1950s, when he worked in collaboration with his partner, Philip A. Moore, Terry's emphasis on harnessing the natural, richly patinated beauty of indigenous timber and stone in his distinctly Modern forms came to define the idiom. Much as Conrad Buff (1926–1988) and Donald Hensman (1924–2002) did during the 1960s and 1970s in southern California, Terry brought a certain organic, rough-hewn elegance to Modern design in his region, especially in his residential designs, from the formation of his first firm in 1946 to his retirement in 1990. As Jim Olson of Olson/Sundberg Architects in Seattle, a leading voice of the subsequent generation of Pacific Northwest architects, observes, "Roland Terry was the man. For residential design at the highest of the high end, no one else came close. He created an environment, a lifestyle, with a sense of history."[1]

From the beginning, Terry worked innovatively and almost always in wood. In 1935–37 he designed a flat-roofed house in Seattle for his mother, the Florence Beach Terry House, while he was an architecture student in his sophomore year at the University of Washington. Its rusticated cedar board-and-batten exteriors and free-flowing spatial interior layout are made warm and inviting through pigment- and beeswax-finished plywood wall paneling and exposed beams. By the late 1950s, his career in full swing, Terry would establish a number of signature design statements, one of which was his use of peeled logs as structural posts, with the timbers left fully exposed as an integral feature of the overall decorative treatment. Whenever pigment was applied to the logs or to the rest of the house's woodwork, it was always a natural color taken directly from the landscape of the site. The result is the same in each house—a comforting setting where the boundaries between indoors and outdoors are largely indistinguishable—as seen at Terry's Jarvis House (1958) in Seattle, where the roof is supported by peeled log columns; the Hauberg House (ca. 1958) on Bainbridge Island; and the Cutler House (1961) in Vancouver, British Columbia. In the house he built for himself on Lopez Island, which he regarded as his dream house,[2] logs are used very assertively.

Begun in 1959 (while Terry was still partnered with Moore) and largely

TOP The single-story side elevation spans 24 feet. The French door on the left side opens to the dining room; the right side belongs to the kitchen. The bench that skirts the edge of the cliff to the left of the house defines a patio space that is protected by the overhang of the flat roof. The 9-foot-high shutters are operable, not merely decorative; their rustic finish results from having been stained with ferric chloride.

BOTTOM The Roland Terry Archive at the University of Washington contains only a few drawings of the house; the documentation is incomplete. This beautiful perspective drawing by Terry, prepared in 1963, depicts an early version of what became the studio. Note the presence of curtains in place of the house's French doors.

The STUDIO at LOPEZ ISLAND
on RICHARDSON COVE in the SAN JUAN ISLANDS
ROLAND TERRY & ASSOCIATES · ARCHITECTS · SEATTLE · W⁵

completed by 1963, the Lopez Island house, which also includes a separate studio building, is a four-bedroom, three-bath arrangement dispersed between two floors that are connected by a spiral staircase. Because the house's lower level is built into the natural drop-off of the cliff on which it is sited, the Terry House looks like a much smaller, single-story cabin from most vantage points on the property. Terry recalls: "This was such a magnificent piece of property that it shouldn't have had anything built on it at all. It should have been left in a completely natural state. With that in mind, I made a point of building the house without cutting down any trees, and designed it to intrude on the landscape as little as possible."[3]

In 1990, when he retired, Roland Terry sold the house, but he was fortunate to find a very sympathetic buyer, who continues to preserve the integrity of the original design.

ABOVE Over a period of several months Terry gathered 17 massive driftwood logs, each about 87 inches in diameter, from the beach below the property. The striking patina on the logs lends a special aura to the building.

RIGHT The living room has 12-foot ceilings, a locally quarried stone fireplace with iron doors, and sliding glass doors that open the room to the patio. Each glass door is 10 feet tall by 9 feet wide. Not a single piece of hardware is visible in the network of hewn-log beams that form the framework of the house. Instead, each beam seems to be held in place by its own very substantial weight. To the right of this space is an additional dining area and, further back, a hall that leads to the master bedroom suite and the lower floors.

OPPOSITE, TOP Although it appears compact because of the low, intersecting ceiling beams, the kitchen is 15 feet wide by 13 feet deep. The cabinets are made of reclaimed old barn wood.

BOTTOM The dining area, just off the kitchen, has reclaimed paneling between the log posts. The floors, like those of the living room, are concrete aggregate, poured after the logs were set. The inlay in the floor beneath the dining table is marble set in an abstract ocean-swirl pattern, a design by artist James Wegner.

ABOVE A view from inside the master bath and changing room. Terry designed simple built-ins for storing linens and other items. The floor is marble.
RIGHT The master bedroom, which overlooks Puget Sound, has reclaimed barn-wood plank walls and its own fireplace.

OPPOSITE This spiral stair off the living room leads to the house's lower floors, where two guest bedrooms, a bath, a wine cellar, and the utility rooms are located. The doorway off the left side of the hall leads to the master bedroom; in the background is the large master bath and changing room.

Brekkestranda Fjord Hotel

LOCATION
Brekke, Norway

YEAR BUILT
1966–80

ARCHITECT
Bjorn Simonnaes

BUILDER
Ingeborg Brekke

STYLE
Organic

This perspective of the elevation that faces the Sognefjord shows how the architect allowed the roofline to be determined largely by the profile of the mountain range visible in the background. The size of the building and the window and door openings suggest lodging for multiple units, but the smaller, freestanding buildings are domestic in scale, like single-family log houses.

Hugging the edge of the Sognefjord in the quaint village of Brekke, some sixty-five miles north of the old city of Bergen on the rugged and highly fragmented coastline of western Norway, is the Brekkestranda Fjord Hotel. Designed by the noted Norwegian architect Bjorn Simonnaes (born 1921), Brekkestranda is unlike any other log building in this book. Its singular Organic Style submits itself so completely to the raw beauty of its setting that even in daylight the architecture is often indistinguishable from the surrounding mountainous landscape. With its peeled log-slab cladding and severely undulating sod-covered roofline, the twenty-nine-room Brekkestranda is one of the most fascinating architectural expressions, timber or otherwise, in all of Scandinavia.

The family-owned log hotel was commissioned in 1966 by the late Ingeborg Brekke, mother of the current owner, Bjorn Brekke, after she resolved to give up accommodating their steady stream of last-minute house guests. "My husband and I were kept so busy putting up travelers who had missed the last ferry to Lavik," she once remarked, "that we thought we might as well build a hotel for them."[1]

The seemingly casual origin of the hotel's inception belies the significance of its ultimate design, which is now widely acknowledged by critics and historians as an integral part of Norway's Organic architecture tradition. Stemming primarily from the works of Frank Lloyd Wright (1867–1959) in the United States and Alvar Aalto (1898–1976) in Finland, Organic architecture has an unmistakable tradition in Norway and includes such major figures of the world of architecture as Pritzker Prize winner Sverre Fehn, Kjell Lund, and Nils Slaato. Its beginnings, however, can be traced to the summer house (1948) that Norwegian architect Knut Knutsen (1903–1969) designed for himself in Portør. Knutsen's design, like the one Brekkestranda would do two decades later, immediately makes an indelible impression through its wavelike skyline, which in some sections nearly scrapes the earth as if it wanted to dissolve itself in the beautiful setting of rock outcroppings. As historian Christian Norberg-Schulz observes, the influence of Knutsen's design was widespread: "Knutsen's pre-ecological concept of architecture was pioneering, and many sought to follow in his footsteps; this can be seen in the establishment of the Wood Prize in 1961, an honor given to those that 'with good architecture call forth those values that yet inhabit wood.' Knutsen was the first recipient."[2]

Although Simonnaes is now reluctant to acknowledge Knutsen's influence[3] in his design for Brekkestranda, there are obvious references to be made, particularly in the freestanding cottages that form the ends of the complex. Brekkestranda distinguishes itself, however, through the deliberately pronounced sense of rusticity and its warmer and more effective embrace of the site. Both aspects are owed in part to the architect's specifying that the rounded outer surface portions typically discarded from milled logs be used as the building's skin (just as Le Corbusier had done in 1952 with his Le Petit Cabanon; see page 116), as well as the thick turf roof.

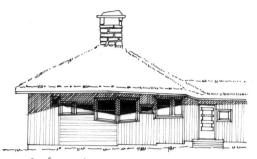

fasade mot syd 1:100

fasade mot vest 1:100

Simonnaes, who studied architecture from 1945 to 1950 at the Academy of Fine Arts in Copenhagen under Steen Eiler Rasmussen, was working as an architect in Bergen when Ingeborg Brekke first contacted him in 1964 to discuss the possibility of hiring him. For much of his career up to that point, Simonnaes had worked almost exclusively in the burgeoning concrete-construction, prefab-housing industry and had become one of its leading voices in Norway with his 1952 invention of Flexihouse, a type of prefab house made of wood. By the time he heard from Brekke, however, Simonnaes was thoroughly disenchanted with the concept of prefab, and he saw in the hotel project an opportunity to make an entirely different kind of statement. As he recalls: "I wondered if it could be a possibility to prove that an antitechnical method of building houses could be even as cheap—and even as good—as any prefab system. I got the chance with a new little hotel near the beautiful Sognefjord. At that time, our architect office had many and great tasks. And very good incomes. We had no fear of the future. I mention this because I am sure you cannot run a risk if you are not safe."[4]

In the 1960s, hotel design—regardless of the scale of the project—was not an area of practice in which a progressive architect could expect to realize radical design concepts. In the case of Brekkestranda, however, Simonnaes found such an opportunity because he was dealing with a very unusual, freethinking kind of client. He recalls that convincing Ingeborg Brekke to accept his design was a relatively simple undertaking, but that it met with considerable resistance within his

OPPOSITE, TOP The south elevation of one of the partially attached cottages in the complex

MIDDLE The west elevation of one of the many freestanding cottages

BOTTOM Perhaps more than any other image of Brekkestranda, this composition, which includes a few of the property's individual cottages, speaks of how masterfully the architecture has been integrated into the landscape. Norwegian architecture buffs should compare it to elevations of Norwegian architect Knut Knutsen's own summer house (1948) at Portør.

RIGHT This viewpoint from under the roof of the terrace shows an entrance to the hotel, with the Sognefjord visible is in the background. Note how the architect protects the entryway to the cottage, undoubtedly because of the occasionally ferocious weather.

BELOW Simonnaes's engaging elevation drawing of the side of the complex that overlooks the Sognefjord. The two houses are connected by a fireproof, concrete-roofed, colonnaded terrace.

BOTTOM Simonnaes's site plan

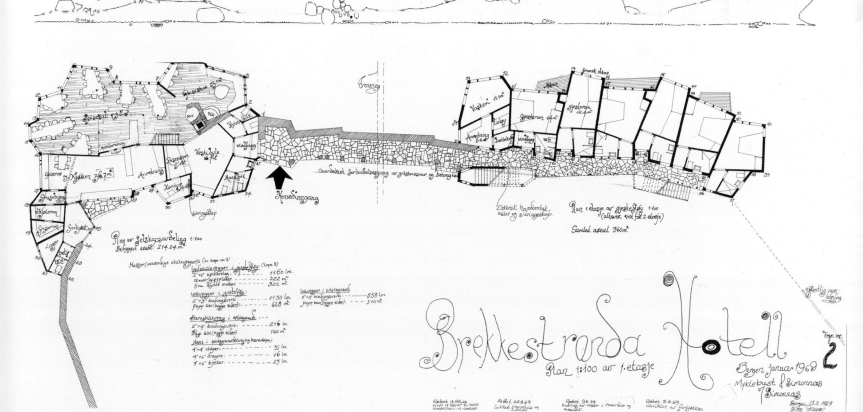

own office. "I made this sketch and sent it to the woman, who wanted to build a very little hotel, or rather a little inn. In a letter I tried to convince her about the need to build one house with kitchen, dining room, and open fireplace room, and another house for the bedrooms. The two houses could be connected with a colonnade with nonflammable concrete roof. I also tried to get her consent to build antirationally with angles awry and with quite different-shaped windows, furniture, and all sorts of things. But first of all, I stressed that the hotel's construction should use natural wood, a turf-covered roof, and roughly built stone walls. The office then divided into two uncompromising camps. One half supported me. The other started at once to make new sketches for an honest, inoffensive hotel. Module-coordinated, of course . . . so that the owner wouldn't risk getting into a bankruptcy right after opening. But it was too late. The owner [Ingeborg] wrote a postcard with these few words: 'Our children are enthusiastic, we are delighted. Start at once.' With that, all retreat was impossible. The project was carried through."[5]

In keeping with Ingeborg Brekke's feisty disposition, she supervised the building of the hotel herself, working alongside the wood craftsmen who had been hired both locally and through Simonnaes's office in Bergen. Once the building was up, she had the bark stripped by hand from its log-slab sheathing. As Bjorn Brekke remembers, his mother remarked after finishing that task: "The hotel looks almost as good as a cathedral!" and proceeded to move on—in the same hands-on fashion—to the next task, that of running the hotel.[6]

ABOVE Taken from the middle of the dining room, this photograph gives one a sense of how the ceiling heights vary from room to room. Note the built-in wall shelving and the way the floorboards are set at an angle, which draws the eye toward the fireplace.

RIGHT, TOP The living room is just off the dining room and has its own fireplace (behind the one shown in the adjacent photograph). By keeping the ceiling height low here, Simonnaes creates a more cozy and inviting space for lounging. The beauty of this room is the composition created by the placement of the log slabs in different directions on the walls and ceiling. Their rich golden patina is very appealing and lends a sense of warmth.

RIGHT, BOTTOM One of the bedrooms in the large building. These rooms are modestly furnished, but it hardly matters, since one's attention is constantly commanded by the fjord, which never ceases to dazzle the senses.

OPPOSITE, TOP Just as Le Corbusier had done with his cabin on the Côte d'Azur for the sake of economy, so Simonnaes specified the use of log-slab cast-offs for the cladding of this frame building. At the time of construction, the bark was still on the logs, but for aesthetic reasons the owner soon began the process of peeling it all off.

OPPOSITE, BOTTOM In the small building shown in the foreground, one can see clearly how the architecture grew out of a locally quarried stone foundation and how the log-slab cladding has been laid both horizontally and vertically.

Koether House

LOCATION
Stetten, Germany

YEAR BUILT
1993

ARCHITECT
Katharina Kölbel

BUILDER
Walter Koether

STYLE
Okanogan Contemporary

The hexagon has a long history of use in both vernacular and high-art residential architecture. Beginning at least as early as 1870,[1] the Navajo Indians of the American Southwest routinely constructed their hogan dwellings (which they fashioned from notched logs) in the shape of a hexagon. In Frank Lloyd Wright's design for the Hanna House (1936) in Stanford, California, the hexagon became the basis of his new unit system called the honeycomb. "I tried that experiment," Wright said, "because I thought that, after all, the square with its angles was not particularly human, not very well adapted to circulation, to moving about in the building. That worked out very well. The hexagon is a very fruitful unit to use."[2] In the instance of the log-constructed Koether House in the small village of Stetten, Germany, the hexagonal shape was chosen not because of any important precedent, but because its designer believed it to be the most efficient spatial use of the owner's small lot.

Koether House is not a typical German log house, or *Blockhaus*, as it is called in Germany. In a *Blockhaus* the logs are hewn square, as opposed to the usual assembly system for log buildings in North America, which uses round, unhewn logs.[3] Although there are exceptions to the rule throughout the world, *Blockhaus* construction, which is widely believed to be of German origin, was historically utilized by those of more significant means, as it requires substantially more labor.

There is little if anything architectural about Koether House that can be traced to purely German origin, however. Instead of referencing the rich tradition of log-and-timber buildings in the Black Forest, such as the sixteenth-century house called Vogtsbauernhof near the town of Gutach, the style of Koether House is inspired by the log houses of the Okanogan region of south-central British Columbia in Canada—an entirely different and much younger tradition.

The earliest extant log houses of the Okanogan region date only as far back as the late nineteenth century. These examples largely reference a single log house, that of homesteader John Douglas, who in about 1872 built one of the region's earliest log houses on record. Although the Douglas House was eventually razed to accommodate the interests of what became Canada's largest cattle ranch, its influence was widespread—as is evident in log buildings that came after it in the region. As Canadian architecture historian Harold Kalman points out, "Douglas's original log cabin and most of the other original buildings have gone, but a number of early-twentieth-century structures spread over a large area tell the ranch's earlier history."[4]

It was while visiting Canada in 1989 that Walter Koether, a German master timber-framer, discovered and promptly became infatuated with the Okanogan's log houses. Not unlike New York's Adirondack Mountain region, this part of British Columbia gave rise to a romantic image of the pioneer log dwelling, which has long

This two-story hexagon efficiently accommodates four bedrooms and two baths. The Douglas fir logs were allowed to settle for about six months before window frames were installed.

been used as a key device of its tourism-based economy, although often enhanced in the process. A number of the Okanogan's historic log houses caught Koether's eye during his stay, and he was also drawn to the contemporary interpretations of these pioneer dwellings that were being constructed as vacation homes. These log homes were a type of contemporary woodsman's house, he thought, one in which he could see himself living. About a year later, still flirting with the idea, he returned to the region and eventually took a job with a local log-building firm in order to study its construction methods in a hands-on fashion.

By 1991 Koether was back home in Germany and ready to transport the notion of the Okanogan log cabin to his native soil. On a prepared plot of land situated near his construction business in Stetten, about sixteen miles east of the city of Memmingen, he hired Baumstamm Haus, a leading German builder of Canadian-style log homes. Baumstamm Haus, working with its Canadian sister company Unique Timber, Inc., of Lumby, British Columbia, put Koether in touch with an experienced German log-house architect, Katharina Kölbel, who was working with the design firm Klafs Planbau in Schwäbisch Hall, Germany. Kölbel would go on to shape Koether's dream house using many of the ideas he had accumulated during his visits to Canada.

Assembled over the period of a year entirely by its owner, the four-bedroom, two-bath hexagonal house made of Canadian Douglas fir logs is included in this book because of the merits of its spatial efficiency. However, it is also worthy of consideration as an example of the far-reaching appeal of the North American log house, especially from Canada, at the end of the twentieth century.

After the house was completed, some of Koether's neighbors began to inquire about its origins, and now there are a number of other Canadian-inspired round-log homes in the Stetten area.

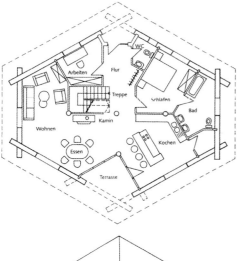

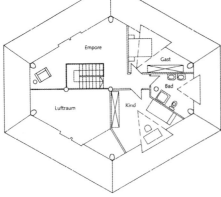

LEFT, TOP The first-floor plan (translation: *Flur* = entry hall; *WC* = toilet; *Bad* = bathroom; *Kochen* = kitchen; *Terrasse* = porch; *Essen* = dining room; *Wohnen* = living room; *Kamin* = fireplace; *Treppe* = staircase; *Schlafen* = bedroom; *Arbeiten* = utility room)

LEFT, BOTTOM The second-floor plan (translation: *Empore* = stair-landing room; *Gast* = guest room; *Bad* = bathroom; *Kind* = children's room; *Luftraum* = loft)

RIGHT, TOP Just past the front door, this view shows the stair to the second-floor bedrooms and, in the background, the kitchen. A finished basement lies entirely below grade.

RIGHT, BOTTOM The dining room and, further back, the living room below the loft. Note the gap in the base of the log post. Inside it is one of the building's many screwjacks, which can be turned to adjust the post's height in case of log shrinkage.

OPPOSITE The Koether kitchen as viewed from the end of the entry hall. The plumbing and electrical work is designed to accommodate any movement of the logs caused by shrinkage.

Ashley House

LOCATION
Gold Hill, Colorado

YEAR BUILT
1993

ARCHITECT
David Ashley

BUILDER
Ed Shure, Timmerhus, Inc.

STYLE
Welsh Farmhouse Vernacular

For Caroline and David Ashley, the purchase in 1990 of 155 acres of high-mountain land in the minuscule town of Gold Hill in Boulder County, Colorado, was the first in a series of steps toward realizing their dream of the ultimate log house for their young family. Firmly determined to raise their children in a small village, they had been looking for a house in Gold Hill, population 210, for many months before luck finally struck them. Land is seldom put up for sale in this unique little place, the site of the first major discovery of gold during the 1859 Colorado Gold Rush. Now that the Ashleys owned what may be the most picturesque plot of land, not just in Gold Hill but in the entire region, David, an architect and an engineer, went about planning the house's design. On every level—architectural design, choice of material, and log construction—he resolved that it would be a personal and finely crafted expression.

In addition to his professional training, David Ashley brought an unmistakable edge to the process of shaping Ashley House. The son of Bernard and Laura Ashley of the venerable apparel and home furnishings company, he had grown up surrounded by good design.[1] His family's rustic East Cottage at the Kent-Surrey border and later, more elaborate homes in Wales and France, would in many respects serve as Laura Ashley's ultimate showrooms, each exemplifying an expression of her calculated design decisions. In the later houses, complemented by hard and soft furnishings produced under the Laura Ashley name, were pieces of his mother's highly pedigreed (and at one time unparalleled) collection of antique furnishings, many of which date to the early days of England's Arts and Crafts Movement. Some of these personalized design environments would end up serving as official images of the company brand, either in capsule form as the design and decoration of its many retail boutiques around the world, or as models of good taste in the how-to decorating books published under the Laura Ashley name.

After completing his degree in engineering and then in architecture, David went to work as an architect and designer for the family business. Eventually, as senior vice president of Laura Ashley Inc., he would oversee the design and construction of some 150 Laura Ashley retail shops across the United States, Canada, and Japan. The experience would all play into his work on the big log house at Gold Hill.

Gold Hill is an exceptional American town in that it appears to have survived the last century with its nineteenth-century innocence intact. A number of its earliest buildings, each dating to the late 1800s and composed primarily of logs in a rough Rocky Mountain vernacular, still stand. There is not a single paved street in the town.

Out beyond the town center, among the thick pines that surround the site on which the Ashley House now stands, it is common to receive wind gusts of up to 100 miles per hour and enough snowfall to make the terrain impassable. As a place for a year-round home, it is not without its formidable challenges, yet the hur-

The symmetrical front elevation with its second-story projection sheathed with board and batten. The architect, David Ashley, is passionate in his belief that architecture should minimize its intrusions on the landscape, and he is quick to point out that this family home is the largest house he has ever designed. It took about 90 days to complete the complex roof, which is surfaced with Thomas Jefferson tiles found in an old barn in western Colorado.

dles placed before the Ashleys by nature appeared minute by comparison to such rewards as the riveting panoramic vistas of the Indian Peaks Wilderness and the Continental Divide, each view obtained from a vantage point situated 8,300 feet closer to the heavens. And so the Ashleys began.

"At one point we had a few gigantic cranes working out here on the mountaintop. The winds would pick up just as they were attempting to lower the logs into place. It was quite a sight," recalls the house's builder, Ed Shure of Timmerhus, Inc.[2] The successful completion of the house, as Ashley made very clear during our interview, would not have happened without Shure's log-crafting expertise. Ed Shure is widely known in the world's vast log-building industry, recognized as something of an eccentric genius and a master craftsman of the highest order. In 1984, on the heels of an extended working tour of Norway and its many historic log buildings, Shure founded the Boulder-based Timmerhus, Inc., a company that has so far completed more than 130 handcrafted log-and-timber structures, its specialty, in various countries. Shure's innovative log-construction methods and frequent use of reclaimed salvage materials have resulted in his becoming influential throughout the log-building world. His unique talents have led to his position as editorial advisor to *Log Home Guide* magazine and made him a sought-after teacher and lecturer for trade groups, including the Timber Framers Guild of North America and the International Log Builders Association.

ABOVE This gable-end detail shows the beautiful contrasting patinas of the board and batten and the old spruce logs.

RIGHT At an elevation of 8,300 feet, the views from the decks are often breathtaking.

OPPOSITE The back of the house accommodates the steep slope of the site with stone piers. The upper deck extends the space of the master bedroom suite, and the lower deck opens off the living room.

As is often the case when an architect who is new to log construction submits plans to the builder, Ashley found that certain adjustments had to be made to his design in order to accommodate the use of logs. "David had his drawings nearly done," Shure remembers with a chuckle, "and then I came and sort of ripped them apart, saying, 'this is what I can do with logs.'"[3] Like a Welsh farmhouse inspired by the classicism of Palladio, Ashley's design is characterized by the symmetrical arrangement of its simple tripartite plan: a full-depth central living hall flanked by equally proportioned bays containing the living room on one side of the ground floor and the kitchen and dining room on the other. On the second floor, the master suite is on one side of the cathedral-ceilinged stair landing and on the other side are the children's bedrooms and bath and a study.

To construct the roughly 5,500-square-foot five-bedroom, three-bath house, which includes a full, finished basement, Shure and his team first had to excavate tons of rock with dynamite. They then laid the house's concrete and native stone foundation, on which Shure crafted the house's richly detailed log structure, using spruce taken from a site north of the Grand Canyon. Each massive tree was stra-

The eat-in kitchen is 23 feet wide by 18 feet deep. With its 9-foot-wide plaster-surfaced fireplace, pine plank floors, granite countertops with recessed copper sink and faucet, and custom windows with wrought-iron hardware, this room is the epitome of rustic extravagance. The dining table is made from a 400-year-old elm.

tegically dropped, often into deep snow, in order to avoid damaging its appearance. "The logs used," says Shure, "were in their natural state from where we got them— they had been dead for at least thirty years—and in the construction of the house we went to great lengths to avoid altering that rich patina."[4]

Visitors to Ashley House, even through this book, can be easily caught up in Caroline Ashley's highly sophisticated selections of furnishings and overall decorative scheme for the interiors. Seated in the living room, where the fireplace warms the Colorado buff stone floor and casts a glow onto each piece of antique wood furniture, the photographer and I found the setting completely enchanting. Nonetheless, one would be remiss not to take the time to admire the graceful architectural efforts and the superlative log work, each of which epitomizes high art.

RIGHT The master bathroom. In the foreground is one of the house's many old plank doors that were reclaimed from a barn in France.

BELOW, LEFT The master bedroom suite, on the second floor, has its own fireplace; the door next to the fireplace opens to the deck.

BELOW, RIGHT The living room, situated just off the living hall, is about 23 feet wide by 22 feet deep and has 10-foot ceilings with exposed, hewn fir beams. The flooring here is Colorado buff stone, with each piece cut in a Dadaist pattern. Perhaps most interesting is the room's fireplace surround, which was reclaimed from a 17th-century manor house in England. All of the Sheetrock work seen here and throughout the rest of the house is cut to follow precisely the lines of the logs.

Neiman Guest House

LOCATION
Deming, Washington

YEAR BUILT
1993

ARCHITECT
David Neiman

BUILDER
Jim Maushak, True Log Homes, Inc.

STYLE
Pacific Northwest Rural Vernacular

At the foot of Mount Baker in the Cascade Mountains, near the icy Nooksack River, is a curious log cabin designed by a young Seattle-based architect named David Neiman. Set far back from the country road that leads to the property and nestled amid a scrub-forest setting of western red cedar, alder, and cottonwoods, this getaway was commissioned by his parents, who live in the traditional log cabin next door. The Neimans wanted a proper guest house, a second log cabin that would comfortably accommodate their children and grandchildren during visits. It was an idea that germinated fortuitously just as their son was finishing a graduate degree program in architecture at the University of Pennsylvania. The getaway cabin project would prove to be an ideal first independent effort for Neiman, a chance to test—on an especially forgiving client—some of his design concepts, particularly those relating architecture to nature. The Neimans' directive to their son, other than that the job be done within their budgetary parameters, was quite open-ended—make it a log cabin.

Historically, the typical log cabin or log house utilizes a simple rectangular or square floor plan, and for good reason. Getting the corner joinery of the logs right is no easy task; better to limit the construction to only what is required. For even in the case of a traditional four-cornered log structure, the construction process usually requires the expertise of a log-home packager because of a general lack of log-crafting expertise in the building industry. In the hands of such specialists, the dried logs are precisely cut and test-assembled at the manufacturing facility. Handling the project like any prefab building, the manufacturer disassembles the kit, packages it, and trucks it to the actual building site for reassembly.

Before configuring his floor plan, Neiman gave much thought to the idea of breaking away from the simple square or rectangle. For the guest house, which would end up being a 600-square-foot, two-bedroom building with one bath, he knew he wanted to go in a different direction. "The original cabin on the property," Neiman points out, "was designed as an iconic log cabin. That was fine. The idea behind the guest cabin was that it was going to have a real link to the landscape, that it would express different ideas spatially."[1]

For Neiman, this specifically meant the utilization of a free-form plan—one whose geometry would be significantly more complex than that of his parents' traditional log cabin. The benefits would include a more open, light-filled living space, which would be achieved by the installment of larger windows, and more of them. Perhaps most significant is that the irregular shape would have wings reaching out into the lush moss-covered landscape to define patio spaces accessed through sliding glass doors, clearly establishing a more open relationship between indoors and outdoors. To make this possible, in order to accommodate the plan's many complex corners, Neiman knew that he would not be able to utilize traditional log construction. Instead, it would be a log-frame hybrid.

As seen from the driveway, the house's complex structure and roof hint at the fact that this is a log-frame hybrid building.

"The construction method was a virtue of necessity," recalls Neiman, who after completing the guest house spent several years with the internationally prominent NBBJ Architects and is now principal of his own successful residential design firm in Seattle. "The log walls are laid out in a series of parallel layers, placed in key locations for spatial and dramatic effect," he points out. "The rest of the walls are filled in using conventional stud-frame construction. Because log walls settle over time as the timbers dry out and shrink, a 6-by-6-foot post is provided in the end of the stud walls wherever they intersect a log wall. Each log is through-bolted to the post to fix it in place and minimize differential settlement."[2] After reviewing Neiman's drawings of the house's construction details, builder Jim Maushak of True Log Homes decided that the complexity of the job merited his hiring Neiman as a carpenter for the job.

Rare is the opportunity nowadays for an architect to assist in the actual construction of his design. It made the process of creating his parents' guest house, where he now stays with his wife and children when they come to visit from Seattle, all the more rewarding. Whereas Neiman takes great pride in having been so hands-on with the making of the cabin, he is quick to point out that the house's success is largely owed to the special relationship he had with Maushak: "I don't think the building would have been possible if the contractor hadn't been located just a couple miles down the road from the site. It made for an unusual opportunity."[3]

Included here as a demonstration of the flexibility of the log-cabin design language, Neiman Guest House also informs us on how to live large in a small space.

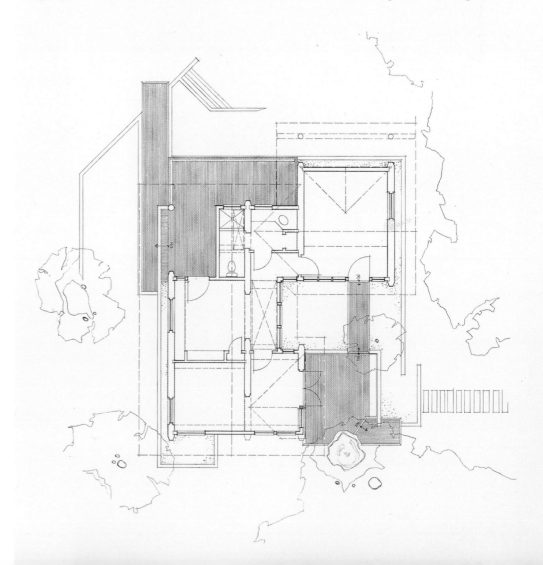

ABOVE Each hand-peeled Douglas fir log is bolted to the framing members and chinked with a latex acrylic polymer for insulation.

RIGHT In this floor plan, each of the patio areas is shaded.

OPPOSITE This front-elevation detail highlights the architect's emphasis on the natural beauty of each material. The battens are Alaskan white cedar; the boards are western red cedar. Note the recessed lighting above the front door.

ABOVE The living room's sliding glass doors open to this patio, which connects to the patio off the large bedroom.

OPPOSITE, TOP LEFT The living room is small, but the high ceilings and many tall windows give it an open feel. The floors are hickory.

TOP RIGHT On most of the surfaces in the bathroom, Neiman used a charcoal porcelain tile that contrasts nicely with the patina of the peeled logs. He also designed the cabinetry. The shower has a skylight.

BOTTOM, LEFT The cuts in the logs allow the natural light coming through the living room's sliding glass doors (just behind this wall) to filter into the small bedroom. During the summer months, the doors are open to admit fresh air.

BOTTOM, RIGHT The windows in this large bedroom look out onto the patio. There is a small loft above the log wall.

Gugalun

LOCATION
Versam, Switzerland

YEAR BUILT
1994 (original structure, 1708)

RESTORATION/ADDITION ARCHITECT
Peter Zumthor

BUILDER
Beat Müller and Zeno Vogel

STRUCTURAL ENGINEER
Jürg Conzett

STYLE
Graubünden "Strickbau"
Farmhouse Vernacular

This vantage point from just below the house allows one to see how Zumthor's team integrated the new roof with the original 300-year-old house. The logs nearest the eaves were appropriated from other parts of the house. The front door is original; note its high position on the façade. The span of the front elevation is slightly less than 23 feet.

Three centuries ago, in 1708, the ancestors of the present owner of this house came to this site, about a dozen miles southwest of the old city of Chur, to lay the stone foundation and assemble the axe-squared log walls that constitute a portion of the building that stands here now. The high-valley location was challenging, situated just below a steep tree-covered ridge, elevation about 3,280 feet. Accessing it from the nearby village of Versam—then and today—was literally an uphill battle, yet it was also a stunningly beautiful place, complete with commanding panoramic views of the Alps that stand above the Safiental basin. It was also a short journey by horseback to the spectacular Rhine Gorge, known as Switzerland's Grand Canyon, where the icy blue Rhine River cuts a sinewy line through this area of the canton of Graubünden.

The tall, gable-roofed farmhouse they built by hand was constructed according to Swiss tradition, using a system of assembly called *Blockhaus*, German for "wood-block house." In the houses of Graubünden, the typical *Blockhaus* features *strickbau*, or knitted, construction. Essentially, this method calls for a log building's walls to be tightly joined at all points of intersection with what constitutes a locking toothed double notch. This allows the walls to effectively support one another. Nails are never involved in Strickbau construction, as they are unnecessary. Typically, as here at Gugalun, the log ends protrude from the façade, indicating where the building's rooms have been "knitted" together.

As in the houses of Graubünden, the logs are left unfinished in order to age naturally, eventually taking on a blackened patina in the areas exposed to sunlight and a rich silvery tone elsewhere. *Strickbau* construction, which is also found in the typical *Blockhaus* of the Wallis canton (with certain stylistic variations, usually evident in the corner joinery), is prevalent in Switzerland. In his book *Switzerland Builds* (1950), G. E. Kidder Smith examined the type, noting that, "Although even the exterior walls are unpainted and unstained, protection against the weather is achieved by four, five, or six inch solid wood thickness. The Swiss actually complain that their stern climate deteriorates wood buildings after four or five hundred years! Paint, they claim, would shorten this life considerably."[1]

Like so many of Switzerland's old log houses that were done in the *strickbau* manner, some of which date to the 1500s, the farmhouse called Gugalun, which means "to look at the moon," survived multiple generations of continued use with little alteration save for patches in the woodwork.

By the late 1980s, however, certain sections of its walls were sagging and the foundation had become fragile. The family member who had inherited responsibility for Gugalun began to consider various ways to go about restoring these and other structural elements of the house, at the same time adding certain mechanical features and amenities, such as a modern kitchen and a bath, all of which would make possible its regular use as a retreat.

Among the most qualified architects in the canton—if not in all of Switzerland—to take on the challenge of working with the nearly three-hundred-year-old Gugalun was Peter Zumthor (1943–), who was based only fourteen miles away in the tiny village of Haldenstein. Appropriately, Zumthor's office was located in a rustic yet very modern barn of his own design. Like most of his completed works, the Studio House (1986), with its sheathing of intricately joined and naturally finished larch-wood slats, closely resembles a finely handcrafted piece of furniture more than an architectural object. In 1987 Graubünden presented him with an award for its design.

Indeed, for his solo works up to this point—which were few—Zumthor had found national recognition as well as international critical acclaim. In 1989 critic Martin Steinmann observed in an essay about Zumthor's output: "It is characteristic of Peter Zumthor's work that his images show a sensitivity for materials and particularly for commonplace materials which give his buildings a strong presence. The buildings can in no way be said to have a borrowed existence; they do not live by referring to something else and therefore do not lose themselves in references as post-Modernist buildings do."[2] Moreover, the Basel-born architect, who as a teenager had apprenticed under his master-carpenter father, had especially deep roots in Graubünden. From 1968 to 1979, after a few years of study at Pratt Institute in Brooklyn, Zumthor held the title of architect in the canton's department for the preservation of monuments. "Zumthor knows intimately the piazzas and arcades of the towns, and the big gabled farmhouses and barns of the countryside throughout Graubünden," Peter Davey wrote in *The Architectural Review*.[3]

Given his expertise and notoriety in Graubünden, it is not surprising that Zumthor was eventually approached to take on Gugalun, although it is astonishing that he took on such a small project in light of the other projects he had in the works.

His design of the addition is nothing but respectful of the nearly three-hundred-year-old original building to which it is married. At the heart of it is a concrete container that his team of builders, led by Beat Müller and Zeno Vogel, embedded in an excavated chunk of the mountainside that existed directly behind the original house. This container allowed Zumthor to expand the building's volume adequately in terms of the client's program, at the same time maintaining the original roof height. As Zumthor says of the effort: "Under a new, shared roof, only the modern essentials were added to the existing structure: a new kitchen, toilet and bathroom, two rooms with larger windows, another wood furnace. We aimed to design a new whole in which the old and new would be assimilated."[4]

Given the importance of materials in Zumthor's approach to architecture, it is not surprising that for the Gugalun addition he chose to take on the challenge of creating an entirely new exterior wall system, instead of utilizing hewn logs, as he would later do (at the client's request) in the case of a single-family house (1997–2003) he designed from the ground up in Graubünden.[5] Thus, rather than competing with the sublime centuries-old log work of the original part of the building, Zumthor honors it through juxtaposition. As the accompanying drawings reveal,

ABOVE A detail of one of the original windows. Note the old strap hinges.

OPPOSITE, TOP This photograph of the house and its owners was taken in 1927.
BOTTOM Zumthor's restoration and the addition place the entrance door to the side, where it is close to the original part of the house. Each window in the addition is protected by a sliding shutter. Unfortunately, it was not possible to open the house during our visit.

ABOVE The addition is seamlessly integrated with the old house. The average dimensions of each of the old hewn logs are 10 to 12 inches high and 6 inches wide. The cornicelike elements on the walls of the addition make the surface more resistant to harsh weather. The new wood is left natural and will eventually take on a patina similar to that on the logs of the old house.

RIGHT Zumthor's section drawing. The original house is on the left in the illustration, with its log walls indicated by darker shading.

OPPOSITE From the road high above the house, a steep path winds down to this point, which offers the first complete view of the house and its site overlooking the Safiental Valley. *Gugalun* means "looking at the moon" in the local dialect.

the new wall system, which is self-supporting, consists of a series of horizontally stacked hollow box-shape beams. Each is assembled by precise joinery and then filled with insulation. Emphasizing the horizontality of the assembly are the batten-like ribs (the bottom portion of each beam), which protrude to give the building's face greater resistance to the elements. They look like logs.

When we arrived at Gugalun, which has no address and was one of the more challenging locations to find on our journey, the photographer and I learned that there had been a miscommunication and that the owner would not be there to open the house for us to take pictures. Fortunately, we were able to examine and photograph the house's exterior, which kept us spellbound for the better portion of a sunny morning. Gugalun, like other works by Zumthor, has an unusual way of captivating the onlooker. Critic Paul Goldberger summarized the feeling best: "Zumthor's buildings, like all great art, make you think of other things, because you want to connect them to the whole of your life experience. You want to be in them, to touch them, to feel how their reality ripples across everything else you know."[6]

Tunebjer House "Vistet"

LOCATION
Torö, Sweden

YEAR BUILT
1998

ARCHITECTS
Anders Landström and Thomas Sandell

STYLE
Swedish Farmhouse Vernacular

Nils Tunebjer fondly remembers the first time he drove from Stockholm with his realtor to see a piece of property on Torö, an island off the rocky Baltic coastline of southeastern Sweden. He was looking for a quiet, remote place on which he could build a vacation home for his family. It was an especially mild summer day with not a cloud in the sky, and as they entered the unpaved driveway that leads into the pine forest by the sea's edge, Tunebjer could see waves crashing on the secluded, pristine beach. A few wet-suited surfers were catching waves in the perennially frigid water, but otherwise no one was around to interrupt the soothing sounds of the surf and the sea breeze entering the forest. The realtor looked over at Tunebjer, smiled, and said, "This is the West Indies of Sweden."

Tunebjer didn't argue the point, and it has now been three years since he erected his log house, or *timmerhus*, as it is called in Sweden, on this very spot. He remains dazzled by the location, and although his choice of house was an unusual one for this long-settled area, it has proven to be equally inspiring and an appropriate decision for the site.

The Tunebjer House, with its rectangular plan, minimally pitched gable roof, eave entry, and walls of squarely hewn horizontally stacked logs (assembled with expertly crafted tooth-notch dovetail joinery[1]), is a modern interpretation of the classic Swedish farmhouse. The prefabricated house, called "Vistet" by its architects, Anders Landström and Thomas Sandell, was originally designed and built as a prototype for a 1998 installation of environmentally friendly houses, a program sponsored by Sweden's Forest Stewardship Council. It was purchased by Tunebjer and subsequently trucked in pieces from the Stockholm exhibition site to Tunebjer's property in Torö. Although prefabrication is often considered a relatively new idea, it was in fact associated with log buildings in Sweden as early as 1880, with the construction of a villa in the town of Lysekil called Storstugan II, the house of Carl Curman, who was its designer and original owner. As historian Barbara Miller Lane observes, "Curman's villa (and others from the 1880s) were built in segments by Ekman's Joinery Workshops in Stockholm and then erected at the site. The Norse revival [the term given Sweden's National Romantic movement] in Sweden was thus closely related to the early development of prefabricated housing."[2]

Vistet's new owner, like so many others who visited the house during the exhibition in Stockholm, had been attracted by the architects' unique fusion of tradition and innovation. Its warm and honest log construction held great romantic and sentimental value for the native Swede, and the functionality of its open plan, its contemporary window sizes, and the portability of its kit-style prefabrication spoke to him both on a practical level and as an admirer of Modern architecture. Moreover, the house is charming without being fussy.

The rear elevation of the three-bedroom, two-bath beachfront house faces the Baltic Sea. The windows are triple glass.

The concepts of simple living and of getting back to nature through the use of organic building materials, says Landström, underscore each major aspect of the design's guiding philosophy. At the time of Vistet's inception, these ideas were in fact prominent in the minds of many Swedes. In Stockholm, a movement was under way—a public yearning for a solution to the problem of too many oversized, environmentally unfriendly houses crowding the landscape. "During the early 1990s," observes Lars Sjöberg, curator at the National Museum in Stockholm and an expert on Swedish historic houses, "a critical scrutiny of developments in the building sector concerning 'sick' houses and poor materials had begun in Sweden. The State Building Society was attempting to regain both aesthetics and durability in housing. Public debates were initiated on the relevance of eighteenth-century designs and materials to modern functional demands."[3]

In Vistet's form and fenestration there appear to be hints of an homage to Villa Erskine (1942–63), the house belonging to Modernist hero Ralph Erskine (1914–2005) in Drottningholm, outside of Stockholm. However, the architects acknowledge only the inspiration of one iconic Swedish house, a recently restored all-log country house called Sörby (ca. 1750), which is located in the province of Närke. Although Sörby and Vistet are strikingly different—the former employs a different log-notching technique, has a saddle roof, and is uniformly symmetrical with its traditional six-room plan—there are some similarities to consider. For example, like Sörby, Vistet has an eave entry and its gable-end log walls reach all the way up to the roof ridge, allowing for second-floor bedrooms behind each gable. Certain aspects of the interiors, such as the whitewashed exposed log walls and the pine plank floors, are handled the same way as well.

In 1994 a replica of Sörby was exhibited on the grounds of the National Museum and became a focal point of the public debates about the modern use of eighteenth century designs and materials.[4] Vistet, designed four years later, was the most noteworthy outcome of that discussion, and it continues to affirm—especially for the Tunebjer family and their guests—that there can be a harmonious interplay between eighteenth- and twentieth-century design concepts in the hands of the right architect. And so the evolution of the Swedish log house continues.

ABOVE Tooth notching is commonly found in old Swedish log buildings. Here the paint scheme highlights the method of construction.

OPPOSITE, TOP The form of this prefabricated house is centuries old, but the window shapes are rooted in the modern era.
BOTTOM The front elevation has an awning over the entrance and a small porch with benches.

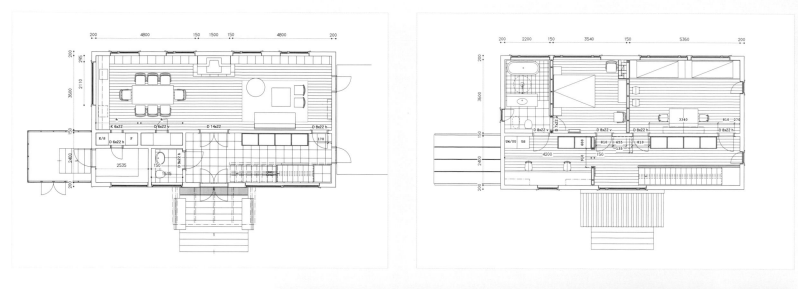

ABOVE, LEFT The first-floor plan shows the entrance giving way to a long hallway, with a bathroom at one side opposite the staircase to the second-floor bedrooms. Further into the house, the eat-in kitchen and living room are in one open area—defined to a degree by the 5-foot-wide fireplace.

ABOVE, RIGHT The second-floor plan shows the arrangement of the three bedrooms and the bathroom, each of which opens off the long stair landing.

RIGHT This is the view as one comes through the front door. Throughout the interior, the hewn logs are painted bright white, which enhances the house's modern character. The fireplace is faced in marble.

OPPOSITE From this position just in front of the fireplace, we see the full depth (just under 12 feet) of the eat-in kitchen. The cabinets have been whitewashed, and the countertop, like the backsplash, is surfaced with oiled steel.

ABOVE This is the smallest of the three bedrooms depicted in the second-floor plan. The partitioning of the rooms is intended to be adjustable, as the inner walls are lightweight and set on tracks.

RIGHT The second-floor bathroom is outfitted with contemporary fixtures. The house's designers are Modernists.

OPPOSITE The living room is next to the eat-in kitchen. The door at the right opens to the staircase of the entry hall.

Heavenly View Ranch

LOCATION
Snowmass, Colorado

YEAR BUILT
1999

ARCHITECT
Robert A. M. Stern

STYLE
National Park Vernacular

The front elevation is faced mainly in stone. The log work is more pronounced inside the house.

ocated ten miles outside world-famous Aspen, the village of Snowmass is a major destination for winter sports enthusiasts, and like so many other resort areas in Colorado, a purveyor of the American West's romantic pioneer log-cabin ideal. In this part of the country, the pioneer log cabin, like iconic images of the silver miner, the ghost town, the cowboy, and the ranch, is a marketing tool of the tourism industry, an integral part of the local cultural mythology.

Since 1968, when the planned community of Snowmass Village was first created in an effort to accommodate the overflow from Aspen, architects have responded to a steady demand for modernized versions of the stereotypical log cabin. On the whole these modern structures run the gamut in terms of style and overall effectiveness, but there is, nonetheless, a certain uniformity shared by most of them. In addition to an intentional exaggeration of scale,[1] a trait that was not common to pioneer log dwellings but evolved in architect-designed log construction, one typically finds a relatively refined interpretation of the crude pioneer vernacular of heavily chinked round-log construction, like that adopted by architects working for the National Park Service.[2] The typical massing, spatial configurations, and details are likewise borrowed from the architecture of the lodges and other buildings of the National Parks, in particular the Craftsman-cum-Adirondack-style Old Faithful Inn (1903; Yellowstone National Park) by architect Robert Reamer, the El Tovar Hotel (1905; Grand Canyon National Park) by Charles Whittlesey, and Bright Angel Lodge (1935; Grand Canyon National Park) by Mary Colter. There are many descendants of these log houses in Aspen, Snowmass Village, and Crested Butte, leading one to assume that if there weren't an indigenous style of log house on the stunning West Elk Mountain Range landscape before the late 1960s, there certainly is one now.

Of all the architects who have made contributions to this new tradition, none has a larger public persona than Yale School of Architecture dean Robert A.M. Stern. His firm in New York City, which has been in practice in its current form since 1977, has created a few of Colorado's most elaborately appointed log houses. Some of them represent traditional log construction, whereas others have utilized hybrid methods of construction. All are relatively large and, as one would expect of Stern, demonstrate a profound awareness of historic precedent.

In an essay from 1981 Stern touches on the philosophy that guides his work and is certainly evident here at Heavenly View Ranch: "For me the pleasure in architecture is not fulfilled merely in the design of buildings and their settings for their own sake—what Le Corbusier ineffably characterized as the 'play of forms under the light'—but requires that those forms incorporate the memory of buildings and their settings from one's own past and from the past in general, from culture."[3]

Stern's work in rustic architecture has produced some exciting designs, although these private houses are not what one typically sees while driving about the area. Quietly built in remote mountainous areas by their privacy-seeking, relatively high-profile owners, Stern's log-house designs—at the request of his respective clients—are an intentionally silent part of his substantial award-winning oeuvre. The stone-and-log-constructed Heavenly View Ranch is one such house.

TOP The rear elevation with its two stories accommodates the slope of the site. The log work references the early 20th-century lodge architecture of the National Park system.

BOTTOM The entry hall gives way to this large open space, which consists of the dining room and, in the background, the living room. From an elevation of 8,700 feet, the windows of both rooms provide spectacular views of the surrounding mountain range. The lighting between each of the king-post trusses was custom made for the house.

OPPOSITE, TOP The site plan shows the winged shape of the house's spatial arrangement.
BOTTOM The living room, with its wide flagstone fireplace and exposed round-log beams, opens onto a broad deck space with mountain views.

BELOW, RIGHT This photograph shows the back end of the dining room; the doorway leads to the kitchen. Note the precision with which the Sheetrock is set in the log framing.

"The house was conceived as a lodge," according to Stern's office, "both in function and design, which would house three generations of a closely-knit family for whom we had built a house in New Jersey ten years before." Built strategically into the side of a ridge in its own parklike setting at an elevation of 8,700 feet, the exceptionally large house is effectively hidden from view as one stands at the front of the property. Stern keeps the fieldstone- and shingle-clad front elevation with its protruding log purlins (horizontal roof supports) low to the earth, its various functions fanned out and organized into wings. This is in keeping with the prescribed design practices of the early National Park architects, as the following passage about Bright Angel Lodge from the United States Department of the Interior's pattern book *Park and Recreation Structures* (1938) suggests:

> No minor part of the satisfaction experienced on viewing that pleasing development is the contribution made by the long, low, horizontal lines of the buildings. Not less than mandatory in that particular location, the low, horizontal feeling there produced would be the appropriate note in almost any natural park setting one could imagine. The advantage invariably deriving from low height is not restricted to grouped buildings as represented by Bright Angel Lodge.[4]

Heavenly View Ranch's combining of round logs (each exposed on the interior) with regular milled studs in its framing is now a popular alternative to full log construction. Although it still retains some of the feel of a traditional log dwelling, the hybrid construction method enables a more flexible floor plan and the use of a greater variety (and larger sizes) of window shapes. This is unlikely to be acceptable to purists, of course, but it continues to grow in popularity, and Stern's persuasive Heavenly View Ranch does much to explain why.

Zajac House

LOCATION
Zakopane, Poland

YEAR BUILT
2000

ARCHITECT
Sebastian Piton

STYLE
Zakopane Style

After he finished his schooling in 1987, the young Polish architect Sebastian Piton knew that he wanted to specialize in shaping buildings in a time-honored manner, using wood and stone. A native of the old city of Lodz, Piton had regularly visited the mountain town of Zakopane in southern Poland, the location of some of the most triumphant works of wood architecture in his country. He fell in love with its log-constructed cottages—the iconic homes of the area's oldest residents, the highlanders—as well as the later houses they inspired, such as the elaborate Zakopane Style log villas of the great Stanislaw Witkiewicz (see page 38). So when it came time for him to set out on his own as a professional, he relocated to Zakopane, where he knew he could live happily and where his ideas about organic architecture would be both fitting and embraced.

Piton devoted most of his early years in this town of 30,000 full-time residents to measuring and closely studying the various features of Witkiewicz's architectural designs. On any given visit to the architect's Villa Koliba (1892) or Dom Pod Jedlami (1897), for example, Piton often found himself sketching on a notepad alongside other local designers doing the same thing.

To a significant extent, Zakopane is still being discovered by the outside world. Although the situation has not yet become widespread, some of the region's long-time residents are now beginning to give in to pressures to sell off at least part of their land holdings. Many visitors to the area want to buy property where they can build a vacation retreat from the ground up and take advantage of the Podhale region's labor force of world-class carpenters and masterful craftspeople. "More often than not," says Piton, "the highlander style, complete with its traditional log construction and woodcarving on the interior and exterior, is what newcomers want for themselves when they build here. From a business point of view, it is obviously very important for local architects to know the highlander culture. Of equal importance is having the old masters to do the finish work, which we still do."

By 1998 Piton's residential designs began to gain recognition, particularly among Zakopane's older locals, for the meticulous way in which he replicated the style's historical defining features and for his introduction of certain structural improvements. These included the devices called screw jacks, which are height-adjustable bolts positioned under the posts of a log building so that the post's height can be raised to compensate for the inevitable vertical shrinking of the logs. It was about this time that Piton met Radoslaw Zajac, the quintessential mountain man and one of Poland's most accomplished professional ice climbers. Zajac wanted a traditional Zakopane Style house for himself and his growing young family to use year round.

For Zajac's one-acre site just outside of town, Piton drew up plans for a rectangular three-level house containing four bedrooms and two baths. Although the

Zajac House is one of the finest contemporary examples of a Zakopane Style log house. Taken from the top of the driveway, this photograph helps to explain why its high stone foundation is a necessity. The front entry is on the landing at the top of the steps.

references to Dom Pod Jedlami are obvious, this house is compact and spatially efficient, designed for twenty-first-century living. In Piton's hands, this has been accomplished without sacrificing any of the qualities that make the Zakopane Style so alluring. Highly picturesque in its form and detail, Zajac House bears all the hallmarks of the style as Witkiewicz shaped it. It appears to grow naturally out of its rugged setting, thanks to its Richardsonian[1] high foundation of locally quarried stone, which is designed to address the heavy accumulations of snow and snowmelt that are common to the mountainside site. (Four-foot piles of snow surrounded the house when we arrived.)

Zajac House also has the distinctive Zakopane roof with multiple half gables—the gable ends highlighted with fancy Podhale-inspired stick work—and decoratively shaped eave brackets. The logs, made of spruce dried for at least two years, are heavily worked in same manner as the prototypical highlander cottages of the region (see page 15). Although the windows appear arched, as at Jedlami, they are in fact standard issue. For economy's sake, instead of specifying custom arched frames and glass, Piton applied wood ornamentation to the windows that suggests an arch.

Anyone who has had the pleasure of experiencing Zakopane is sure to recognize that many fine contemporary examples of the Zakopane Style log house are to be discovered in the area. The overall refinement of Zajac House—its design, materials, and construction—is especially outstanding, however. The work of Piton and his team of builders and craftspeople suggests that, when the Zakopane Style finally finds greater awareness outside this beautiful but isolated place, the Zajac House will be among the primary sources of reference that architects turn to in drafting their interpretations of it.

ABOVE This detail of the front entrance provides a nice view of the house's abundance of carved ornamentation—all examples of Tatra Mountain highlander motifs.

RIGHT Piton's preliminary perspective drawing for the Zajacs includes a garage to the left of the front entrance. Otherwise, the house was constructed as originally conceived.

OPPOSITE The symmetrical rear elevation with its projecting half-gable at the center

ABOVE Between each spruce log are minuscule wood shavings called *welnionka*, which are made specifically for this kind of construction by the local highlander master craftsmen. In Zakopane log construction, the wood is always left to age naturally.

ABOVE, RIGHT As seen here in the living room, the beautiful log work is left exposed throughout the house. The turned post to the right of the fireplace is mounted on a screwjack, which can be used to compensate for any shrinkage-related movement of the log beam above it.

RIGHT The den on the second floor, right next to the children's bedrooms

OPPOSITE This is what one sees after passing through the foyer. The staircase fits into a tight space, but note the turk's-cap lily carvings on the baluster panel. The level of design detail in the house is extraordinary. Sheepskins are a common decorative feature in Zakopane.

Midnight Canyon Ranch

LOCATION
Montana

YEAR BUILT
2003

ARCHITECT
Kelly F. Faloon, Colbert & Faloon Architects

BUILDER
Yellowstone Traditions

INTERIOR DECORATOR
Lynn Glenn McAtee

STYLE
National Park Vernacular

Midnight Canyon is one of the most beautifully and remotely sited houses in the book, with the nearest sign of commercialization hours away. Technically speaking, this is the back of the house.

In designing this wing of the house, the part that contains the great room, architect Kelly Faloon was heavily influenced by the grandest examples of lodge architecture in the National Park system.

"**D**uring one of my first research visits to the site, I climbed to the top of this particular butte," says architect Kelly Faloon as he leads us—camera equipment and all—up a steep incline behind the complex of log buildings he designed. "That day, I had a near face-to-face encounter with a black bear." Directing our attention to a nearby pattern of unnervingly large bear tracks, he was obviously not simply having fun at our expense. This part of Montana, more remote than any other we visited for the book, is home not only to black bear but also to mountain lion and other potentially dangerous neighbors of the four-legged and winged varieties. "It's a real working ranch, which is what the owner wanted," he adds. Indeed, from the amphitheater-like setting to its natural inhabitants to the log architecture that Faloon conceived for it all, Midnight Canyon Ranch, although new, has an unmistakable air of authenticity.

Like so many others who have built themselves log homes, the owner of Midnight Canyon Ranch, a resident of Greenwich, Connecticut, had spent quality time in a pioneer-type log cabin when she was growing up. Indeed, the image of that log cabin situated on the working ranch in Montana where she learned to ride horses (eventually becoming an accomplished rider) had long occupied a special place in her memory. Toward the end of the 1990s, when her children started to have their own children, she finally resolved to create a place in the country for her family that would be as special as the one she had known. It would be the real thing, a working ranch with horses, a ranch manager, log architecture, and natural scenery to take one's breath away.

Finished in 2003, Midnight Canyon Ranch's 6,000 square feet of living space stretch out over a small portion of the ranch's 5,000 acres, located in the vicinity of Yellowstone National Park. The sprawling main house and the freestanding building that serves as the garage have corrugated-metal roofs and are constructed primarily of Montana fieldstone and kiln-dried lodge-pole pine logs from Canada. The logs feature end-only hewing, which recalls the entrance station at Yellowstone National Park.[1] The small, freestanding, sod-roofed guesthouse farther up the site's slope is a renovation of an old line shack (a small building, typically made of logs, that cowboys of the nineteenth century would build on the open range to use as a shelter when weather became severe) that was in a dilapidated state when the owner bought the property. Faloon restored its old structural log work, all of it square hewn, and gave it a new roof and an additional room, which became its kitchen.

Although it can be very difficult to reach during the winter months, the ranch is designed to be used throughout the year. In shaping his floor plan, Faloon paid particular attention to the idea that at times the house would be used by only a few people, although its primary purpose would be to accommodate—as privately as possible—the owner's large family and occasional guests (often all at once). Thus,

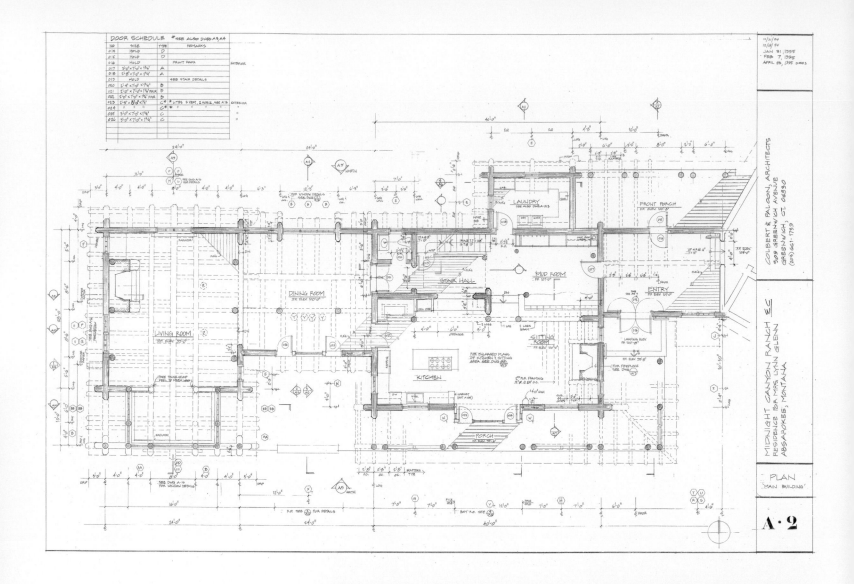

COLBERT & FALCON, ARCHITECTS
309 GREENWICH AVENUE
GREENWICH, CT. 06830
(203) 661-1759

MIDNIGHT CANYON RANCH
RESIDENCE FOR MRS. LYNN GLENN
ABSAROKEE, MONTANA

PLAN
"MAIN BUILDING"

A·2

the central part of the house, with its southerly facing porch—the part Faloon calls the middle house—consolidates all necessary functions into a highly functional two-story zone. In this way, its second-floor master-bedroom suite, the ground-floor family room, kitchen/dining area, and guest bathroom can be closed off from the two wings (the guest bedrooms in one, the formal dining room and Great Camp type great room/hall in the other), allowing for more efficient energy consumption and easier upkeep. Another significant benefit from his handling of the floor plan, a signature Faloon statement, is that the house's interiors reveal themselves dramatically in stages. Connected to the middle house by hallways, the two distinctively designed wings appear to have been added over a period time, a common practice with houses of homesteaders and other pioneers.

The forms employed by Faloon in the design of the three-part main house derive from multiple sources and styles. The south-facing elevation of the middle house with its eave entry and broad, covered porch recalls the Dutch Colonial farmhouse-inspired Big Trees Lodge (1932) designed by architect Eldridge T. Spencer at Yosemite National Park, California.[2] However, Faloon has improved it by adding dormer windows, which allow the exposed logs of the interiors to be bathed in natural light. The wing that holds the four guest bedrooms and baths—the wing connected to the middle house by the entry hall—echoes any number of handsome, utility-oriented ranger's cabins in the National Parks. The other wing, which is at the western end and contains the dining room and great room, is Midnight Canyon's grand architectural gesture. Here Faloon incorporates ideas from the Great Camps of New York's Adirondack Mountains, in particular the late-nineteenth-century log cottage of the original Kamp Kill Kare on Sumner Lake.[3]

Faloon's greatest achievement in the design of Midnight Canyon Ranch, however, is his acknowledgment of the house's setting. Too many log houses have a small number of window openings. Not here. As one passes through the house from room to room, the variations in floor level and window height show an overriding concern for dramatically framed views of the surrounding cliffs and the valley. As we learned during our trek up the cliff behind the house, there is much to take in. Some of it, including the black bear, is probably best seen from the safe confines of the log house.

ABOVE, TOP The structural logs of the wing containing the great room frame beautiful views of the landscape.
BOTTOM Lodge-pole pine that has been saddle-notched with end-only hewing and then chinked and stained

OPPOSITE, TOP This is a section of the house's floor plan. Missing is the guest wing, which branches off from the entry.
BOTTOM This 19th-century line shack, which sits between the house and the cliff, was here when the owner first bought the property. Faloon rehabilitated the structure, restoring its square-hewn log construction and installing plumbing so that it can be used as a guesthouse.

RIGHT The kitchen and breakfast table shown here are in the central part of the house. In the background is a staircase that leads to the second-floor master bedroom, children's rooms, and bathrooms. Visible at the far left is a doorway that connects the kitchen to the formal dining room.

BELOW, LEFT The formal dining room is situated between the kitchen and the great room. Faloon deliberately placed the windows unusually high on the wall to provide dinner guests with clear views of the cliff behind the house.

BELOW, RIGHT This is the main room of the line shack. A small kitchen is located to the right. Notice the heavily distressed floorboards.

OPPOSITE The great room also has high windows so that the butte can always be viewed from inside.

Lanzinger House

LOCATION
Brixlegg, Austria

YEAR BUILT
2003

ARCHITECT
Antonius Lanzinger

BUILDER
Antonius Lanzinger with Konrad Merz of Merz, Kaufmann & Partners

STYLE
Modern

"One hundred years ago in the Tyrol region," remarks Antonius Lanzinger as he leads us through the front door and into the *Stube*, or living room, of his home, "this method of construction was the norm." Lanzinger is referring to the *Blockhaus* type of log building, which uses logs that have been hewn square. Precise handcraft is inherent to proper *Blockhaus* construction, especially in the Austrian state of Tyrol, a feature that obviously resonates strongly with Lanzinger, formerly a professional carpenter and now an architect of buildings that are at once respectful of the region's old rustic-design traditions and emblematic of high-art Modernism. His chosen method of construction indeed predates the twentieth century, comparable in certain fundamental ways to the original 1708 *strickbau*-style *Blockhaus* construction of the log house known as Gugalun (see page 162).[1] But the overall design, a flat-roofed towerlike form with unusually positioned slender voids cut out as in a piece of sculpture, strongly suggests architecture of our time. It just happens to be made of logs.

Located in the quiet mountainside village of Brixlegg, about thirty miles from the capital city of Innsbruck, Lanzinger House is the first house designed by the young architect for himself and his family. Before settling in Brixlegg in 2001 to begin its construction, a task he handled mostly himself, Lanzinger lived in Innsbruck. There he had attended the University of Innsbruck's prestigious school of architecture, studying closely the teachings and the architecture of Josef Lackner (1931–2000). A lauded professor of architecture at the university from 1979 until the late 1990s, Lackner also maintained a thriving practice and, although largely unknown in the United States, has long been regarded as a hero of late Modernism in Austria. In Innsbruck he realized many thrilling buildings, including St. Norbert Church (1969–71), Ursuline Convent and School (1971–79), and, most prominent of all, the Amthorstraße Apartments (1990–92), a building specially designed to give each of its individual units abundant sunlight through the winter. It is in Lackner's residential designs, mostly outside of Innsbruck, in particular the Berger House (1972) in Aldrans and Schweizer House (1980) in Oberperfuss, that one can see the fearless tradition out of which Lanzinger's design ideas grow. Also in 1972, in the Leygraf House in Zell am Moos (outside Salzburg), Lackner completed an extensive exterior and interior restoration and renovation of an eighteenth-century *Blockhaus*. Lackner's show of respect for its historic log shell, while at the same time bringing its interiors and mechanical components into the present, would not have gone unnoticed by Lanzinger.

In the Tyrol, the mountainous topography is extremely jagged. On any given day it is riveting to look at, but only about 14 percent of this landscape can be built upon. For architects like Lanzinger, the sense of obligation, of responsibility to society, minimizes their intrusions on what little bit of land is available. Lanzinger House's

In Austria and Switzerland especially, architects on the cutting edge are utilizing log construction to stunning effect, often for themselves. This is Lanzinger's west-facing front elevation–a veritable showcase of carpentered precision. The door opens to the living room.

vertically oriented spatial organization, the rooms stacked one atop the other, is therefore a responsible strategy. It is also a solution to the problem of building into the lower side of a mountain, an area with a 35-degree slope that is often shaded from direct sunlight during the winter months when the sun is especially low in the sky. The tower shape, of course, has a long history here and can be seen in any number of medieval castles sitting high on the land between here, Switzerland, and northern Italy, such as the twelfth-century Castle Tirol near Merano.

Lanzinger House's quiet façade grows out of a poured-concrete shell that is embedded in the rock of the mountainside. Each of its window openings, as Lanzinger points out, is positioned and sized to permit not a panoramic view but a predetermined, edited one. Natural light pours into the rooms in startling, invigorating ways—usually from high on the wall but always according to plan. In log-house design, this strategy of handling fenestration can be traced at least as far back as 1952, when it can be seen in Le Corbusier's Le Petit Cabanon (see page 116) at Roquebrune-Cap-Martin, France. In a part of the world where stunning landscape views can be had by looking in practically any direction, it is noteworthy that Lanzinger House's warm and inviting interior spaces are intentionally designed to be concerned only with what is happening indoors. There is not a single attempt in the design to blur the distinction between indoors and outdoors, as we have seen in Richard Neutra's Helburn House (see page 108) in Bozeman, Montana, for example, another house designed for a snowy climate.

Lanzinger House's combining of historicism with overt Modernism might put off those who have grown comfortable with the more prevalent, traditional notion of the log house (the gabled roof over round-log construction with standard symmetrical window and doorway arrangement). Moreover, seen in the context of Brixlegg, a place full of contemporary Tyrolean-style chalet spin-offs, some might mistakenly

ABOVE, TOP The house's square-hewn fir log walls have full dovetail joinery. At each corner, running through the full height of the building, are bolts that reinforce the log work.
BOTTOM The square-hewn logs are tongued and grooved lengthwise for a locking fit when stacked.
RIGHT The section drawing at the left shows the mechanical core and chimney that runs through the tower; the one at the right reveals the vertically oriented spatial flow.

OPPOSITE Lanzinger's house has the distinction of being the only towerlike structure in his community and the only house that does not lie in the depressing shadow of the mountain from which this photograph was taken.

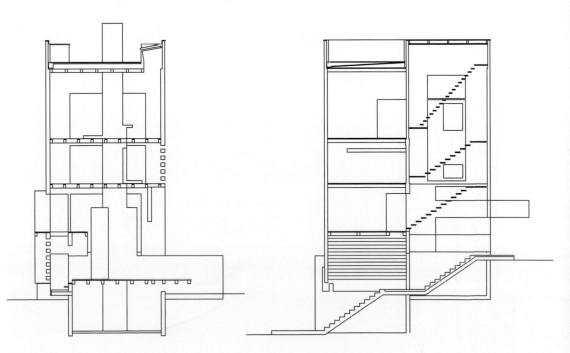

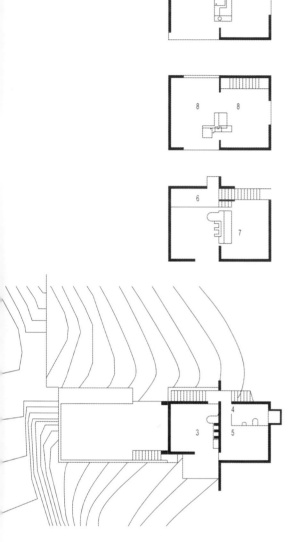

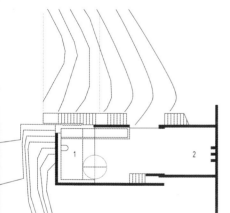

LEFT The top illustration depicts the roof deck. Note that on each floor is a centrally positioned fireplace.
Key:
1. toilet
2. workshop
3. *stubbe*, or living room
4. bathroom
5. den
6. gallery
7. kitchen
8. children's bedrooms
9. master bedroom and informal living room

ABOVE The master bedroom and the shower stall that stands between the bed area and an informal living room with fireplace. The windows behind the Lanzinger−designed bed are the top row at the front of the house. Above the painting is a skylight. The ceiling is clad in 4-x-8-foot sheets of plywood. Behind this vantage point is a massive pivoting door that opens to a small balcony overlooking the mountainside.

view Lanzinger House as an anomalous work for its location. In fact, this house belongs here, perhaps more so than its neighbors. As critic Daniel Fugenschuh observed, Modernism merged early and successfully in the Tyrol within the context of the region's time-honored rustic building traditions:

> In the 1920s, pioneering architects of the Tyrol chose to take the Modern Movement to the most remote valleys of the eastern Alps, where they defined a new architectural language. By combining local techniques and cultural traditions with the International Style, architects such as Baumann, Welzenbacher, Mazagg, and Holzmeister not only produced several noteworthy buildings, but also sought to refine the alpine topography with their architecture, equaling the quality of more widely known examples from Switzerland.[2]

In 2003, the year of its completion, Lanzinger House was awarded the prestigious Holzbaupreis ProHolz Tirol, which is given each year for outstanding architecture in wood. Seen from the valley below the steep hillside site, the house is immediately noticeable. Eventually, however, Lanzinger House's fir logs will begin to take on a blackened patina from exposure to the sun, which will allow it to blend in with the deep greens of its striking natural surroundings—just as Lanzinger intended.

BELOW, LEFT The kitchen island and the fireplace, which is 8 feet wide. The window in this room is positioned high on the wall so that sunlight will also reach the gallery, which is just behind the right side of the fireplace.

RIGHT The *stubbe*, or living room, is open to the gallery next to the kitchen and can be entered from the front and back of the house. In accordance with the region's traditions, this is the primary gathering place—the area where one receives guests. Lanzinger also designed the table and chairs. The orange tiled surface is the stovepipe of the heating system that extends through to the top of the house.

Savage House

LOCATION
Driggs, Idaho

YEAR BUILT
2003 (original log portion, 1902)

ARCHITECT
Kurt Dubbe, Dubbe Moulder Architects

INTERIOR DESIGN
Smash Design

BUILDER
Dan Pauroso, HP Woodworking

STYLE
Anglo-Western Pioneer Vernacular

The form of Savage House, the front of which is shown here, is relatively simple. What makes the house such a spectacle is the supreme effectiveness of the integration of old and new elements in its design. It comes down to homeowners' willingness to let the designers use only deeply patinated, reclaimed wood. After spending time here, one has to be reminded that this is largely a new house.

ABOVE A detail of the old portion's square-hewn spruce logs with dovetail joinery

OPPOSITE This photograph gives a clear sense of the complete house and its context.

Before one reaches the old-fashioned ranch gate at the bottom of the Savages' hilly stretch of land, it is necessary to pass through the picturesque Teton Valley, a rural, mostly flat expanse between two breathtaking mountain ranges, the Tetons and the Big Hole Mountains. The sixty-two-acre Savage property—which sits near the foot of Grand Teton (elevation 13,770 feet)—is then accessed by a long uphill approach, which offers only a partial, teasing glimpse of the house at the top of the rise. At the final, dramatic turn in the unpaved driveway, just beyond a cluster of pines, the house's façade comes into full view. With its site-appropriate scale and its palette of weathered reclaimed red oak board and batten, spruce logs, hand-split cedar shakes, native Rocky Mountain stone, and red oak clapboard, all aglow in late-winter afternoon sunlight, the Savage House presents itself as an idyllic expression of the notion of the rustic home.

Consisting of a relatively modest 2,500 square feet, the house's architecture, design, and construction are the result of a collaborative effort, principally between Kurt Dubbe of Dubbe Moulder Architects of Driggs, Idaho, and Jackson Hole, Wyoming; Harper Welch and the late Marc Clements of Smash Design of Seattle, Washington; and Dan Pauroso of HP Woodworking, also of Driggs. Since their formation of Dubbe Moulder Architects in 1994, Chris Moulder and Kurt Dubbe have established themselves as leading designers of historically accurate rustic architecture, much of it involving log construction.

The story behind the house's log section is a bit more complex than the rest, since it originated a century earlier, in about 1902. The log portion alone, specifically the first story and a half of it, originally constituted a freestanding dwelling attached to a homestead property in Jackson Hole. When Dubbe found it, the house was owned by the grandson of the original homesteader, who was faced with having to demolish it to make way for a new building needed for the business that he operated on the same property.[1] A historic preservation specialist as well as an architect of new buildings, Dubbe quickly concluded that the old log homestead could be reborn as an integral part of his new project for the Savages. After the family enthusiastically agreed with him, the log house was acquired and trucked intact over the Teton pass (elevation 8,431 feet) to Driggs. When it got as far as the property's uphill approach, however, the house had to taken apart in order to make it to the top of the driveway. That's when its history began to emerge.

"They used old newspaper for insulation. Newspaper and wallpaper—just add another layer every fall. There were probably fifteen or twenty layers of wallpaper," recalls builder Dan Pauroso, who handled the process of disassembling the house and putting it back together.[2] One piece of insulation, the front page of the *Kansas City Tribune*, was dated 1902. By taking apart the old house, to which a full second story would eventually be added, Pauroso was able to see how proficiently the log

work had been done. "The joinery . . . was impeccable; they were very accurate. I was pretty amazed at how flat everything sat," he recalls, "and how it went back together."[3] That the building's logs had been hewn square, their corners joined in a half dovetail notch, makes the century-old log house a rare example of its kind for this part of the United States, where round-log construction is most common among buildings from that period. Furthermore, it suggests that the log work—all of it hewn by hand—may have been done by an immigrant from Russia, Scandinavia, or Finland.[4]

The integration of the original 1902 log house with the additions that flank it—a small board-and-batten-sheathed sun room on one side, the stone-clad single-story kitchen wing on the opposite side, and the clapboard-faced garage wing at the east-facing far end—could easily have appeared forced. But the result seems natural in the Savage House, thanks in large part to the architect's choice of materials (much of them taken out of an old tobacco barn in Tennessee) and his decision to give the roof of each wing a different pitch. Another key factor, of course, is the skillful handling of the new openings that had to be made in the century-old log walls.

To position the front door where it is now necessitated cutting the old logs and fitting a completely new doorframe into the log courses. Most of the old structure was left intact, however, with the original doorways being used to access the sun room on one side and the kitchen on the other. The plan's circulation also feels natural, a surprise in a building with so many spatial components.

The Savage House design's overriding concept, like that of Midnight Canyon Ranch (see page 188) and Orcas House (see page 210), suggests that, as in typical pioneer-era houses, the house grew in stages as its owners attained greater financial footing in the community. In the United States, where our history is relatively young, there is an increasing desire among homeowners to create a house with the appearance of longevity of place, of rootedness. Reclaimed building materials are gaining in popularity, for example. Although the result is something of a manufactured reality, in principle this is a laudable practice, in that it honors the built traditions of our forefathers. When done correctly, as in the Savage House, the house appears to belong to its site. As more and more Americans come around to this idea, we may finally see the much-needed disappearance of the so-called log McMansions—those unsightly and severely out-of-scale log homes that appear to have been built without any regard for their setting.

OPPOSITE Smash Design handled the interiors, including this space, the sunroom. The 9-foot-wide fireplace is faced in marble, and the floors are polished concrete (note the logs slices in the floor).

RIGHT On the other side of the sunroom's fireplace is the living room, shown here. The aluminum spiral stair leads to the master bedroom.

OPPOSITE The garage wing's media room has plywood paneling on the walls and ceiling. An Adirondack Style baluster distinguishes the staircase that takes one to the guest bedrooms. Note the hewing marks on the stair's risers.

RIGHT The guest bathroom next to the kitchen is likewise full of eye-catching details. The walls are made of wormy chestnut planks.

BELOW The wall of the kitchen behind the 1950s General Electric refrigerator belongs to the original log house. To distinguish the wall from the rest of the structure, the designers left it unpainted. The countertops rest on custom-made steel-framed cabinets that have vintage postcard images, one of Jackson Hole and one of Yellowstone, decoupaged onto their fronts. The cabinet framing and dimpling of the plywood recalls the work of Charles and Ray Eames's Case Study Program shelving of the 1950s.

Orcas House

LOCATION
Orcas Island, Washington

YEAR BUILT
2004

ARCHITECT
Mira Jean Steinbrecher

BUILDERS
Unique Timber and Needham Construction

ENGINEER
Jennifer Anthony, Beaudette Consulting
Engineers

INTERIOR DESIGNER
Bristal Design Group

STYLE
Craftsman

The 36,000-acre Orcas Island, part of the San Juan Island chain off the coast of Bellingham, Washington, has some of the most pristine natural scenery in all of the United States. Accessible from the mainland only by boat or plane, the place has indeed a remote, quiet beauty. To build appropriately here is to build unobtrusively, allowing nature to inform the design wherever possible. In their selection of Mira Jean Steinbrecher, a noted architect of Whidbey Island, Washington, the owners of Orcas House believe they were able to accomplish just that.

The outcropping of rock that reaches up some two hundred feet into a forest of madrona trees, providing panoramic views across emerald-green Puget Sound, immediately struck one of the owners of Orcas House as the only plot on which to build. Although it was one of the first properties she was shown on Orcas during her search, she felt an immediate connection to the place. Since childhood she had dreamed of having a log home one day, and the location she had created in her mind so many years ago was not unlike the one she had just found.

After she brought her husband to Orcas Island and allowed him to be similarly seduced by the site, the couple invited Steinbrecher out to determine whether it could accommodate the elaborate kind of log house they had expressed interest in building. Steinbrecher, too, became enamored of the area, and with her expertise in designing environmentally sensitive, earthquake-resistant log houses, several on challenging mountainside sites, she knew that, although it would not be easy to build on Orcas—not to mention on one of its remote, undeveloped spots—it could be done. Soon, the seven-acre plot was acquired and the design process got under way.

"Mira Jean made a strong impression on us by requesting that, before she began her work on the design of the log house, she would visit us at our primary residence in California," recalls the owner. "She came out for the weekend and studied how our family lives, how we use that house. The success of the log house owes much to this."[1]

Armed with a clear understanding of her client, along with the array of magazine clippings of favored designs and several pages of detailed requests, room by room, that they had submitted to her, Steinbrecher returned to her drafting board on Whidbey and went about the process of shaping what would become a very substantial log house.

With its multiple projections capped by low-pitched gabled roofs, their wide bargeboards (the boards that hang from the projecting end of a roof) protecting the structure's exposed log purlins (the horizontally laid members that typically rest on rafters to support a roof) and at the same time enhancing the shadow depth of the extended eaves, Steinbrecher's design derives from the language of the Craftsman Style. There are a number of surprising touches, including the addition of board and batten to the exterior surfaces of stone, log, and shingle, with each of the woods

The front elevation, as seen from the driveway that meanders up the hilly site

stained a rich madrona tree reddish-brown in order to harmonize with the site. Appropriately, board and batten is the dominant sheathing material of the "working" portions of the house, the wing that contains the garage and workshop. "I . . . love to use mixed finishes to really play with shadow and texture in my buildings. It keeps them from becoming overwhelmed by horizontality," says Steinbrecher.[2] Another prominent characteristic is its additive massing, which has the effect of suggesting the house grew in stages over time. Most importantly, the plan conforms to the natural contours of the site. Thus, despite its considerable size, the architecture submits itself to this beautiful place.

Among the many attributes of this 6,100-square-foot house that cannot be seen from the outside is the design's accommodation of Unique Timber's state-of-the-art log-building practices. Each of the logs (spruce is used throughout except for the upright logs, which are Douglas fir) was vacuum-kiln dried, which allows for the desired core-moisture content and leads to reduced shrinkage later on. As a representative from Unique Timber explains: "Logs that go through our kiln drying process will not experience a further reduction in diameter. Logs that have been kiln dried are firmer and have greater structural integrity than either green or standing dead logs. As a result, there is less compression at the notches and joints than would normally be expected. The result is a significantly reduced overall log wall compression of 1 to 2 percent."[3] Steinbrecher's design was made to accommodate up to a 4 percent loss in building height because of log shrinkage.

In this part of the United States, earthquakes and high winds are not uncommon. As Steinbrecher explains, her design is acutely aware of these potential challenges:

> The bottom course of logs is firmly tied to the first-floor platform and the foundation. Then vertical hardwood dowels are staggered throughout the log walls to act as "drift pins," or shear pins, to take the lateral loads. (By the way, in these islands, winds often end up creating more lateral load than earthquakes!) Finally, the roofs are securely lagged to the top-wall logs and roof structure to prevent them from sailing away from the uplift of gusting winds.[4]

Orcas House is also a completely wired "high-tech house," the only one featured in this book. An elevator connects the finished basement's "tech center" with the two-car garage and, on the top floor, the workout room and sauna.

For those who seek a traditional log house, one with all of the luxurious appointments normally associated with the latest high-end homes in America's suburbs, Orcas House is a model to be emulated.

ABOVE The log walls are assembled with beautifully executed full-scribe joinery with saddle-notched corners.

OPPOSITE, TOP LEFT The rear elevation with its deck that reaches 24 feet out from the house toward Puget Sound. The house's logs are stained to match the bark of the nearby madrona trees, such as the one in the foreground of the photograph.

TOP RIGHT The covered porch of the front entrance. The copper gutters release to chain-link drains instead of traditional drains.

BOTTOM As the house's highly detailed floor plan illustrates, log home construction in the 21st century often involves high technology.

ABOVE The patio, with its wonderful view of Puget Sound, is just outside the master bathroom.

RIGHT, TOP The master bathroom has limestone floor tiles, marble tops on the two vanities, a separate shower finished in limestone and lit by a skylight, and a freestanding soak tub.

RIGHT The house's beautifully crafted log work is full of subtle details, such as this arched opening between the kitchen and the pantry.

OPPOSITE The living room fireplace is 15 feet wide at its base and has a built-in cabinet for audio-visual equipment. The floors, like the kitchen and dining room, are done in reclaimed white oak. Notice how the corbelled logs of the wall at the left help support the massive logs of the ceiling structure. In the background are the dining room and kitchen. The second-floor stair landing is also visible from this viewpoint.

OVERLEAF The kitchen and dining room are gathered in one large space for purposes of entertaining. The countertops are granite, except for the bar surface, which is teak. The open shelving is all cantilevered. To the right of the dining table is a 12-foot-wide sliding glass door, which opens to the aforementioned rear deck.

Draper Cabin

LOCATION
Hancock, New Hampshire

YEAR BUILT
2004

ARCHITECT
Daniel Vincent Scully, Scully Architects

BUILDER
Richard Pisciotta

STYLE
Deconstructivism

Architect Dan Scully's cutting-edge design for the lakefront summer cabin utilizes the idiom of the log cabin, not its log architecture. In the south-facing elevation (or the front of the house), shown here, one gets a clear view of his penchant for juxtaposing materials. The corrugated steel works here only because of the presence of the cobblestone chimney and the log siding. Considered as a whole, it is a highly engaging composition.

Architect Dan Scully recalls how each time Tom and Ellen Draper and their young children visited his office to discuss ideas for the expansion of the family's lakefront log house and to look at the models he had made, the children would invariably get hold of the intricately assembled mock-ups and knock them out of square. The design of the multi-building addition was in progress at the time, and, like Scully's models in the hands of the children, ideas were still being tossed about. In the end, remaining true to his typically witty and metaphorical approaches to shaping buildings,[1] Scully found concepts in the children's adjusted versions of his work—notably, a series of parallelograms (originally rectangles)—that would ultimately govern the house's plan.

Scully, who started his own architecture practice in 1981, was at one point associated with the phenomenon called Carchitecture, a playful style of design that looks to automobile culture for visual cues. The architect's Route 101 Two-Lane Highway Home (1981) in Dublin, New Hampshire, has a kitchen shaped like the hood of a Pontiac. For Nelson Elementary School (1990) in Munsonville, New Hampshire, Scully created a building in the shape of a choo-choo train. His work's emphasis is in fact more wide-ranging aesthetically, however, and includes the 1999 renovation of a barn (ca. 1884) on Blow-Me-Down Farm, the property on which Augustus Saint-Gaudens lived and worked in the Cornish Art Colony of Cornish, New Hampshire; the Bellows Falls Waypoint Interpretive Center (2003) of the Connecticut River Scenic Byway in Bellows Falls, Vermont; and the Aron Library Wing (2003) at Marlboro College in Marlboro, Vermont. The common thread in all of Scully's architecture, as he points out, is the aim to create places with which the user can identify.

In the *Abrams Guide to American House Styles* (2004), historian William Morgan points out that, in general, "Deconstructivist houses defy proportional canons," that a "sense of multiple, clashing, or oddly interlocking forms predominates."[2] As with that icon of Deconstructivism, architect Frank Gehry's own house (1978; a renovation) in Santa Monica, California—with its surfaces of plywood, corrugated metal, and chain-link fencing—such a description applies to the forms and materials of the main house of Draper Cabin. This two-story portion of the complex is clad in sheets of shiny corrugated metal and log siding. It is a wood-frame structure, the front elevation of which, in form and fenestration, bears some resemblance to the prototypical New England barn. But its utilization of pre-twentieth-century precedent largely stops there. The rest involves reinvention.

From his office in Keene, New Hampshire, Scully described the complex as "four structures of sliced and diced logs, corrugated steel, and boulders."[3] There is obviously more to it, however. In the screened gazebo's deconstructed log corner posts (what he calls "stacked Tootsie Rolls") and in the manner by which Scully merges the rectangular plan of the original house with the tapering parallelograms

of the addition, there exists an prime example of how far the notion of the "log cabin" evolved at the beginning of the twenty-first century.

Whereas purists are prone to find anything but full log construction outside the boundaries, for many others the log house has long connoted much more than a traditional building type with a rigidly defined method of construction. In the United States, as in Norway, Finland, Sweden, Switzerland, and several other nations, the log cabin is loaded with patriotic symbolism. That kind of power has allowed it to morph into a pliable aesthetic—one that can be used constructively or decoratively, in part or in whole. Some might say it has become a style, a design language. This notion is manifested in the buildings of the Draper Cabin to a greater degree than any of the other houses in this book that use log cladding over a traditional milled-lumber frame.

Scully's appropriation of "log cabin-style" 2-by-8-foot eastern white pine log siding for the main house is his way of paying homage to the site's original cabin, the vernacular of the region, and the tradition of the log cabin in general. However, by harnessing the log cabin idiom only for selected portions of his overall scheme, Scully instills the desired sense of rusticity, warmth, and connection to site without having to subject his design's form and plan (both of which are radical in relation to log construction of today) to the restrictions of traditional log construction. Here, for example, typical considerations of full log construction, such as log settling, corner configurations, and notching strategies, are non-factors.

THIS PAGE, TOP The south-facing elevation, with the lake to the left of the house
BOTTOM The west-facing elevation, which overlooks the lake. The site's original cabin is the ground-floor portion of the end of the building, at the far right in the drawing.

OPPOSITE The complexity of this house makes the inclusion of a floor plan an absolute necessity. First of all, one must bear in mind that the lake is situated in the area that occupies the right side of this page. The south-facing elevation is at the top of the page, and the small freestanding screened gazebo and studio buildings (not shown in the plan) sit only a matter of yards away.

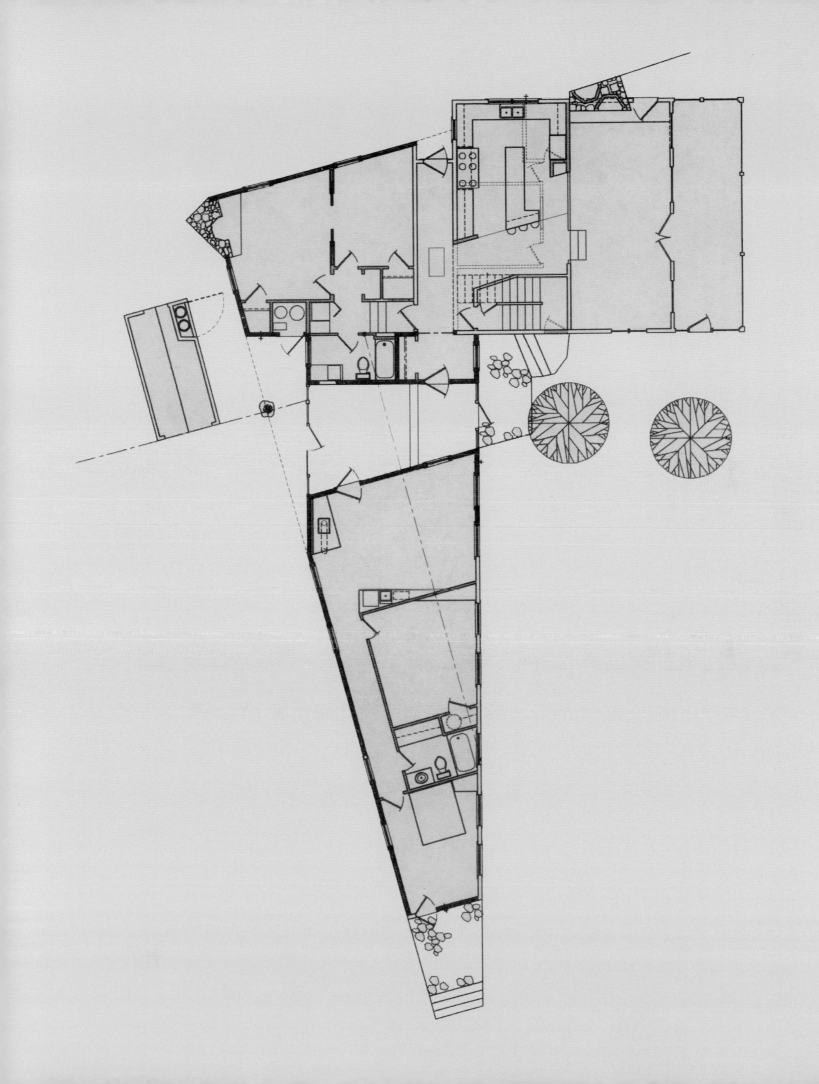

ABOVE The screened gazebo's front elevation incorporates what Scully refers to as "sliced and diced logs." Like on the house, the logs are 2-x-8-inch eastern white pine "log cabin siding," each stained brown to match the color of the original cabin's logs.

OPPOSITE Another view of the unusual screened gazebo. The main house's south-facing elevation is in the background, with the lake located to the left.

Although the rusticity of the design is achieved through the dark brown log cladding (also left exposed on the interior), the house's contemporary feel owes much to the portions of the building that are clad in industrial-looking panels of shiny silver corrugated steel. The result is a contrast between old and new—one that gives the house a greater overall visual complexity and excitement. One might argue it does so without forfeiting the feeling of warmth that is common to a traditional log house. The Draper Cabin has the look and feel of a log cabin.

The buildings of Draper Cabin, a total of 3,630 square feet distributed between the renovated and enlarged main house with its new attached guest wing, along with the new studio building and screened gazebo, sit in a camplike arrangement on about three lakefront acres a half-mile's drive into deep woods. The project marks the first time that this architect, whose father is noted architecture historian Vincent Scully, ever worked with logs. In 2005 the American Institute of Architects, New Hampshire, awarded Scully its Excellence in Architecture Honor for the design.

RIGHT This fireplace in the living room is one of two in the house. Notice the skylight. The floors are fir.
BELOW The door of the south-facing elevation opens to a hallway, which is visible behind this room, the kitchen. The trusses of the roof structure are left exposed here to contrast with the surfaces of the bare pine plank, the corrugated metal, and the brown logs. Off this room is a staircase that leads to the second-floor master bedroom.

OPPOSITE The second-floor master bedroom. The windows in the background look out onto the lake.

LOG JOINERY TYPES

Double Notch

Full-dovetail

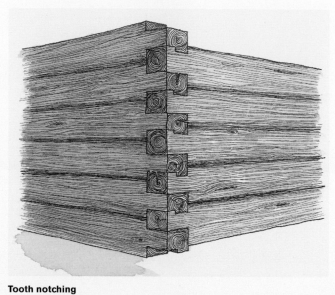

Tooth notching

Semilunate

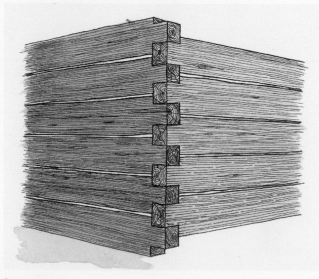

Square Notch

"V" Notch

Half Notch

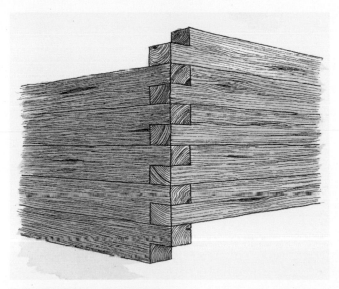

Half-notched false corner timbering

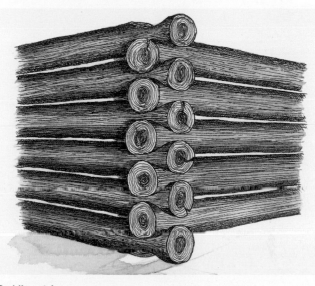

Saddle notch

Half-dovetail

Scribed and grooved chinkless wall

NOTES

Introduction

1. Richard Guy Wilson, contributor, "America's Castles: Adirondack Camps" (New York: A&E Home Video, 1995). Documentary film.

2. http://burlingamepezmuseum.com/classictoy/lincoln.html

3. Dell Upton, *Architecture of the United States* (New York: Oxford University Press, 1998): 136.

4. See Calder Loth, ed., *The Virginia Landmarks Register, Fourth Ed.* (Charlottesville: University Press of Virginia, 1999).

The Log House and the World's Fairs

1. See Henry C. Matthews, *Kirtland Cutter: Architect in the Land of Promise* (Seattle: University of Washington Press, 1999).

2. Ibid.

3. Ben Macomber, *The Jewel City* (San Francisco: John J. Newbegin, 1915).

4. Historic American Buildings Survey, Library of Congress, Washington, D.C.

Frögnerseteren

1. After a great fire in 1624, Oslo was renamed Christiana for Christian IV, but in 1925 the city's name was changed back to Oslo.

2. Holm Hansen Munthe is cited as the originator of the Dragon Style in George Eliassen, *Norwegian Architecture throughout the Ages* (Oslo: H. Aschehoug, 1950): 258; and in Christian Norberg-Schulz: "Munthe, Holm" Grove Art Online. Oxford University Press, August 10, 2005, http://www.groveart.com.ezproxy.lapl.org/.

3. Barbara Miller Lane, *National Romanticism and Modern Architecture in Germany and the Scandinavian Countries* (Cambridge: Cambridge University Press, 2000): 62.

4. Swiss and Stick are essentially the same; each is typically characterized by a rectangular plan set in a two- to three-story light frame structure, the upper stories slightly overhanging, with a steeply pitched multi-gable roof featuring numerous decorative trusses in addition to wide overhanging eaves supported by exposed brackets, wooden siding applied in multiple patterned directions and often raised from the wall surface for greater emphasis, covered porches with abundant spindle work, turned posts, and balustrades with decoratively perforated infill panels, and windows that were significantly larger than was previously customary in residential design (among Scandinavians, large windows were a very important development).

5. Christian Norberg-Schulz, *Nightlands: Nordic Building* (Cambridge and London: MIT Press, 1996): 126.

6. Ibid., p. 127.

7. Christian Norberg-Schulz: "Munthe, Holm" (2005). Schulz suggests that the Dragon Style culminated in the Art Nouveau-inspired design by Norwegian architect Henrik Bull for Norway's dining hall at the 1900 Exposition Universelle in Paris.

8. Eliassen, *Norwegian Architecture throughout the Ages* (1950): 258.

Ravine Lodge

1. A Great Camp can be defined as a rurally sited, multi-building residential complex—typically a central lodge and use-specific dependencies, each of log construction—intended for seasonal recreational use.

2. See Craig Gilborn, *Adirondack Camps: Homes Away from Home, 1850–1950* (Syracuse: The Adirondack Museum/Syracuse University Press, 2000): 125.

3. See John Zukowsky, ed., *Chicago Architecture 1872–1922: Birth of a Metropolis* (Chicago and Munich: Art Institute of Chicago and Prestel Verlag, 1987).

4. See Tom L. B. Sloan, "The Architecture of William W. Boyington," M.A. thesis. Northwestern University, 1962.

5. See I. D. Guyer, *History of Chicago: Its Commercial and Manufacturing Interests and Industry* (Chicago: Church, Goodman & Cushing, 1862).

6. See Sloan, "The Architecture of William W. Boyington."

7. Susan S. Benjamin, *An Architectural Album: Chicago's North Shore* (Winnetka: Junior League of Evanston-North Shore, 1988): 132.

Dom Pod Jedlami

1. Zbigniew Mozdzierz, *The House Under the Firs: The Pawlikowski Family Residence* (Zakopane: Doctor Tytus Chalubinski Tatra Museum, 2003): 327.

2. As with the folk houses of Japan, the historic log-constructed highlander cottages in Zakopane are distinguished more by their roof shape than by any other feature. The half-gable form, which is characterized by the gable ends having hips at the ridge line and at the eave level, is the key overall characteristic. Interestingly, other than Poland's Podhale region and a few small villages in Slovakia just across the border from Zakopane, we have found this roof shape dominant only in the early log-constructed folk houses of Gutach, Germany, and in various villages throughout Japan. For more on the Japanese Minka, see Chuji Kawashima, *Japan's Folk Architecture: Traditional Thatched Farmhouses* (Tokyo, New York, and London: Kodansha International, 1986).

3. Author e-mail interview with the Tatra Museum's Zbigniew Mozdzierz, June 2005. Translated by Magdalena Olsen.

4. Jan Zachwatowicz, *Polish Architecture* (Warsaw: Arkady, 1968): 379.

5. See Mozdzierz, *The House Under the Firs*.

6. Translated for the author by Magdalena Olsen.

7. Author e-mail interview with Mozdierz, June 2005. Translated by Magdalena Olsen.

8. Ibid.

9. Ibid.

10. Author e-mail interview with Mozdierz, August 2005. Translated by Magdalena Olsen.

11. The house's guestbook contains these names, along with their various laudatory comments about the house.

Hvitträsk

1. See Barbara Miller Lane, *National Romanticism and Modern Architecture in Germany and the Scandinavian Countries* (Cambridge: Cambridge University Press, 2000).

2. Recently, as of 1991, Karelia was officially divided between its two bordering nations, with the Finnish parts designated as the Region of North Karelia and the Region of South Karelia and the Russian-owned portion known as the Republic of Karelia.

3. See Paul Oliver, ed., *Encyclopedia of Vernacular Architecture of the World* (Cambridge: Cambridge University Press, 1997).

4. Richard Weston, *Alvar Aalto* (London: Phaidon Press, 1995): 11.

5. Villa Wuorio, located in Laajasalo, Finland, was commissioned shortly after GLS established their first office together in 1896, while the young architects were still attending the institute. The house was completed in 1898, the year they won the competition to design the Finnish Pavilion, an Art Nouveau-style building, for the Paris Exposition of 1900. Villa Wuorio has ornately carved baroque window surrounds and walls of squarely hewn logs that are decoratively corbelled at the ends. It remains in good condition.

6. See Koti Taideteoksena, *Hvitträsk: The Home as a Work of Art* (Helsinki: Otava Publishing Company, 2000).

7. Ibid., p. 119.

Tallom

1. Henrik O. Andersson and Fredric Bedoire, *Swedish Architecture: Drawings 1640–1970* (Stockholm: Byggforlaget, 1986): 160.

2. Lars Israel Wahlman, *Verk Av L I Wahlman* (Stockholm: AB Tidskiften Byggmästaren, 1950): 194.

3. Barbara Miller Lane, *National Romanticism and Modern Architecture in Germany and the Scandinavian Countries* (Cambridge: Cambridge University Press, 2000): 174.

4. Ibid., p. 64. Sweden's entry at the exposition, a replica of the fifteenth-century farmhouse Ornasstuga, was a two-story gabled structure with a cantilevered gallery and a peculiar spiral staircase that linked the house's gallery-sheltered porch to the second floor. Norway's submission consisted of a large version of one of its medieval loft buildings, a building showcasing *reisverk,* or "raised work," a combination of stave and log construction.

5. Ibid., p. 103.

6. Wahlman, *Verk Av L I Wahlman* (1950): 66.

7. Ibid., p. 194.

Clubhouse, Stickley Museum at Craftsman Farms

1. See Mark Alan Hewitt, *Gustav Stickley's Craftsman Farms: The Quest for an Arts and Crafts Utopia* (Syracuse: Syracuse University Press, 2001): 11.

2. Hewitt's book offers an exhaustive look at the rise and ultimate demise of Stickley's Craftsman Farms.

3. Gustav Stickley, *More Craftsman Homes,* reprint ed. (New York: Dover Publications, 1982): 147.

4. Ibid., p. 146.

5. Despite historians' suggestions to the contrary, in the United States there is the perception that the log cabin is America's original house type. For more on this subject, see Harold R. Shurtleff, *The Log Cabin Myth: A Study of the Early Dwellings of the English Colonists in North America* (Gloucester, Mass.: Peter Smith, 1967).

6. Stickley, *More Craftsman Homes* (1982): 146.

7. In June 1913, about a year after Stickley published his endorsement of the log house in *More Craftsman Homes,* *House and Garden* magazine published a feature called "The Revival of the Log Cabin" by Georg Brochner.

8. Stickley, *More Craftsman Homes* (1982): 146.

9. See Mary Ann Smith, *Gustav Stickley: The Craftsman* (New York: Dover Publications, 1983): 110.

10. See Hewitt, *Gustav Stickley's Craftsman Farms* (2001).

11. Ibid., p. 12.

Power House

1. Diane Maddex and Alexander Vertikoff, *Bungalow Nation* (New York: Harry N. Abrams, 2003): 14.

2. The Grand Canyon Hotel closed in 1958 and destroyed by fire in 1960).

3. Letter on Yellowstone Park Hotel stationery from Robert C. Reamer to "Mr. C. B. Power, Helena, Mont." dated December 5, 1910. Collection of Pat O'Connell Anderson, Bungalow Bed and Breakfast, Wolf Creek, Montana.

4. Letter dictated by phone from Reamer to "RMS at Mammoth" and sent to Power on Feb. 7, 1911. Collection of Pat O'Connell Anderson, Bungalow Bed and Breakfast, Wolf Creek, Montana.

5. Letter from Reamer to Power, February 24, 1911. Collection of Pat O'Connell Anderson, Bungalow Bed and Breakfast, Wolf Creek, Montana.

6. Ruth Quinn, *Weaver of Dreams: The Life and Architecture of Robert C. Reamer* (Bozeman, Montana: Leslie and Ruth Quinn, Publishers, 2004): 82.

7. Ibid.

8. Author telephone interview with Pat O'Connell Anderson, December 2005.

9. Quinn, *Weaver of Dreams* (2004): 83.

Semmering House

1. Adolf Loos, "Architektur," *Der Sturm* (1910).

2. Wolfgang Pehnt, ed., *Encyclopedia of Modern Architecture* (New York: Harry N. Abrams, 1964): 177.

3. See Mario Schwarz, "Fin-De-Siècle Country Houses at Semmering," available on the Internet at: http://www.fwf.ac.at/en/finals/final.asp?L=E&F_ID=6002740&file=c:%5Cwebsite%5Csite%5Cen%5Cfinals%5CP13959E.html

4. This house is extant and can be viewed on the Internet: http://www.zacklimmo.com/se.html

5. The archives of Adolf Loos are in the Albertina Museum, Archive of Architecture, Vienna, Austria.

6. Reprinted in Adolf and Daniel Opel, *On Architecture: Adolf Loos* (Riverside, Calif.: Ariadne Press, 2002): 122–23.

7. Panayotis Tournikiotis, *Adolf Loos* (New York: Princeton Architectural Press, 1994). 113.

Log House

1. Esther McCoy, *Five California Architects* (New York: Reinhold, 1960): 153.

2. Virginia L. Grattan, *Mary Colter: Builder upon the Red Earth* (Flagstaff: Northland Press, 1980): 14.

3. In log construction, "pen" is the term used to describe a structure composed of four log walls fastened together with corner notching.

4. The Prairie Style is here treated as a part of the Modern movement. As historian H. Allen Brooks has outlined, it comprised the hallmarks we have come to accept as being Modern: "Every feature of the building—from the basic mass to the smallest detail—was clear, precise, and angular. Ornament, per se, was a rarity; enrichment was dependent on the textural expression of materials and the often lively juxtaposition of various shapes and forms. Only in the stylized or abstract patterns of the leaded glass (or zinc strip) windows did one find consistent ornament. The historical styles, as commonly known, were rejected." H. Allen Brooks, *The Prairie School: Frank Lloyd Wright and His Midwest Contemporaries* (Toronto: University of Toronto Press, 1972): 5. For more on the beginnings of Modernism, see William J. Curtis, *Modern Architecture Since 1900* (London: Phaidon Press, 1982).

Villa Vekara

1. For more on Aalto's sauna designs, see Göran Schildt, *Alvar Aalto: The Complete Catalogue of Architecture, Design and Art* (New York: Rizzoli, 1994): 76.

2. According to Schildt, built examples of these homes exist in the Savonmaki and Konopelto districts of Varkaus, in Kauttua on Varkaudemaki hill, in Sunila's Puistola area, and in Noormarkku.

3. Markku Lahti, "Alvar Aalto and the Beauty of the House," *Alvar Aalto: Toward a Human Modernism* (Munich, London, and New York: Prestel Verlag, 1999): 49.

4. Göran Schildt, *Alvar Aalto: The Early Years* (New York: Rizzoli, 1984): 169.

5. Schildt, *Alvar Aalto* (1994): 179.

6. In March 2005, intending to photograph Villa Kihlman for this book, we traveled to the village of Kuru on Lake Näsijärvi, where we met with a number of the town's officials, including Kirsi Riijioja, and a local architect to discuss the status of the house. They had no knowledge of its existence, and we were unable to locate it independently.

Hellman House

1. See http://www.kcet.org/about/station-history/index.php?ID=2. The television station's Web site offers a summary of Charles Ray's contributions to film, including his company's work in architecture and design: "We at KCET remember Charles Ray as the man whose company built the handsome Spanish-style red brick studios and offices that are still in use on the property today." The as-yet-unknown set designer of Charles Ray Productions during the years 1922–23 is likely the original designer/architect of Hellman House.

2. Ibid.

3. Lay's production company had built two additional log houses for the film, and they too were seized by Hellman and relocated to his three lots in Rustic Canyon, where they remain today. However, no documentation exists to suggest that the other two received remodeling by an architect after the relocation.

4. Betty Lou Young, *Rustic Canyon and the Story of the Uplifters* (Santa Monica: Casa Vieja Press, 1975): 79.

5. This is supported by documentation authored by Rustic Canyon historian Betty Lou Young, contained in the Alfred Heineman archive at the Greene and Greene Archives division of the Huntington Library in Pasadena, California.

6. Author telephone interview with Randy Young, director of the Pacific Palisades Historical Society in Pacific Palisades, California, December 2005. Young, whose research of the Hellman House is the most extensive on record, also says the house is the oldest surviving movie set in California.

7. This is according to documentation from a 1971 interview with Alfred Heineman, conducted by historian and Heineman Brothers expert Robert Winter and on file at the Alfred Heineman archive.

8. Author telephone interview with Steve Pauly, grandson of Arthur Heineman, December 2005.

9. Robert Winter, ed., *Toward a Simpler Way of Life: The Arts and Crafts Architects of California* (Berkeley, Los Angeles, and London: University of California Press, 1997): 138.

The Point (formerly Camp Wonundra)

1. Linda Flint McClelland, *Building the National Parks: Historic Landscape Design and Construction* (Baltimore and London: Johns Hopkins University Press, 1998): 94.

2. Eliza Scott Harris, "Call of the Wild," *Departures.com*, September 2002, http://www.departures.com/tr/tr_0902_adirondacks.html

3. Ibid.

4. Harvey H. Kaiser, *Great Camps of the Adirondacks* (Boston: David R. Godine, 1982): 136.

5. Craig Gilborn, *Adirondack Camps: Homes Away from Home, 1850–1950* (Syracuse: Adirondack Museum/Syracuse University Press, 2000): 259.

6. Kaiser, *Great Camps of the Adirondacks* (1982): 69.

7. The completion of Camp Minnowbrook (1948), a Distin design at Blue Mountain Lake, is generally acknowledged as the end of the Great Camp era.

8. Craig Gilborn, *Adirondack Furniture and the Rustic Tradition* (New York: Harry N. Abrams, 1987): 67. For a complete listing of Distin's work, see Gilborn, *Adirondack Camps* (2000): 311–14.

Helburn House

1. Author interview with Julius Shulman, January 2005, Shulman House and Studio, Los Angeles, California.

2. Thomas S. Hines, *Richard Neutra and the Search for Modern Architecture* (Berkeley and Los Angeles: University of California Press, 1982): 126.

3. "Weeping brick" is an early twentieth-century masonry construction method that allows the wet mortar between each brick to seep over the edges and onto the wall surface of the bricks before drying to create a shadow-casting rustic look. "Board and batten" refers to closely spaced boards with narrow wood strips covering the joints, usually applied vertically.

4. Richard Neutra, *Richard Neutra on Building: Mystery and Realities of the Site* (Scarsdale, N.Y.: Morgan & Morgan, 1951).

5. Time Magazine Archive, "Homes Inside Out," *Time*, vol. XLIX no. 5, (February 3, 1947): http://www.time.com/time/archive/preview/0,10987,886332,00.html

6. Ibid., p. 299.

7. Ibid., p. 270.

8. John C. Brittingham, "Historic Houses: Neutra in Montana," *Architectural Digest* 61, no. 6 (June 2004): 50–54.

9. The spiderleg outrigger is a single roof-support beam that is extended at least a few feet beyond the eave to connect with a freestanding post positioned in the landscape, resulting in the perception that architectural space has been stretched into nature.

10. Author interview with Dion Neutra, October 2005, Neutra House and Studio, Los Angeles, California.

11. Brittingham, "Historic Houses (2004): 50–54.

Le Petit Cabanon

1. Peter Adam, *Eileen Gray: Architect, Designer* (New York: Harry N. Abrams, 1987): 310.

2. Le Corbusier would eventually design for Rebutato a series of connected single-room rental cabins, which are still at the site, right across from the preserved L'Etoile de Mer building.

3. Adam, *Eileen Gray* (1987): 310.

4. Sarah Menin and Flora Samuel, *Nature and Space: Aalto and Le Corbusier* (London and New York: Routledge, 2003): 95.

5. In *Nature and Space*, Menin and Samuel point out that, over a considerable period after Le Corbusier drew the basic form, the cabin design actually had input from five colleagues, including Jean Prouvé.

6. Willy Boesiger and Hans Girsberger, *Le Corbusier: 1910–65* (Basel: 1967): 291.

7. Bruno Chiambretto, *Le Corbusier à Cap-Martin* (Marseille: Editions Parantheses, 1987): 39–42.

Pearlman Cabin

1. Author interview with Nancy Pearlman, February 2005.

2. Alan Hess, *The Architecture of John Lautner* (New York: Rizzoli International Publications, 1999): 42.

3. Author phone interview with Helen Arahuete, November 2005.

4. It is on this ground, then, that the subject of the Lautner House on Lake Superior is raised for discussion in the text.

Terry House

1. Justin Henderson, *Roland Terry: Master Northwest Architect* (Seattle and London: University of Washington Press, 2000): 37.

2. Ibid., p. 111.

3. Ibid., p. 113.

Brekkestranda Fjord Hotel

1. Atle Skjelde, "A Hotel in a Class of its Own," *Seasons of Norway* (spring-summer 2000): 46.

2. Christian Norberg-Schulz, *Nightlands: Nordic Building* (Cambridge and London: MIT Press, 1996): 179.

3. Author telephone interview with Bjorn Simonnaes, November 2005.

4. Bjorn Simonnaes, "Lekture 9: An Attempt to be Conscious about the Architectural Revolution in these Days." A lecture given in November 1981 in Dundee, Edinburgh, and Glasgow. Unpublished, this lecture exists in the archives of Simonnaes and was shared with the author by him.

5. Ibid.

6. Atle Skjelde, "A Hotel in a Class of its Own," *Seasons of Norway*, Spring/Summer 2000, p. 46.

Koether House

1. *Random House Webster's College Dictionary* cites 1870–75 as the "date of first written occurrence" of the Navajo hogan building type.

2. Bruce Brooks Pfeiffer, ed., *Frank Lloyd Wright: His Living Voice* (Fresno: The Press at California State University, 1987): 184.

3. Author interview with master log-home designer and builder Ed Shure of Timmerhus, Inc., in Boulder, Colorado, January 2005.

4. Harold Kalman, *A History of Canadian Architecture,* vol. 1 (New York: Oxford University Press, 2006): 413.

Ashley House

1. See Anne Sebba, *Laura Ashley: A Life by Design* (London: Weidenfeld and Nicolson, 1990).

2. Author telephone interview with Ed Shure and David Ashley, April 2005.

3. Ibid.

4. Ibid.

Neiman Guest House

1. Author telephone interview with David Neiman, November 2005.

2. First published on www.neimanarchitects.com

3. Author telephone interview with David Neiman, November 2005.

Gugalun

1. G. E. Kidder Smith, *Switzerland Builds: Its Modern Architecture and Native Prototypes* (New York and Stockholm: Albert Bonnier, 1950): 24.

2. Martin Steinmann, "On the Work of Peter Zumthor," *Domus* 710 (November 1989): 52–53.

3. Peter Davey, *Peter Zumthor: Carlsberg Architecture Prize 1998* (Copenhagen: Carlsberg, 1998): 6.

4. Peter Zumthor, *Peter Zumthor Works: Buildings and Projects, 1979–97* (Baden: Muller, 1998).

5. This house is featured in the book *Swiss Made: New Architecture from Switzerland* (2003) by Steven Spier with Martin Tschanz. Along with another house featured in the book, a design by Swiss architect Gion Caminada that was built in Graubünden in 2000, Gugalun demonstrates the ongoing relevance of the *strickbau* method of log construction.

6. Paul Goldberger, "Swiss Mystique," *Vanity Fair* (July 2001): 108–15.

Tunebjer House "Vistet"

1. One of the earliest extant examples of this kind of notching can be found at the church at Petäjävesi, Finland, which was built about 1763, during the time when Finland belonged to Sweden.

2. Barbara Miller Lane, *National Romanticism and Modern Architecture in Germany and the Scandinavian Countries* (Cambridge: Cambridge University Press, 2000): 64.

3. Lars Sjöberg, *The Swedish House* (New York: Monacelli Press, 2003): 43.

4. The Sörby replica, whose construction of which was overseen by Lars Sjöberg, senior curator at Stockholm's National Museum, went on to be installed in several locations, including Jamestown, New York, as "The Swedish Design House," and it served as a showcase for eighteenth-century Gustavian Style (1772–1809) furnishings.

Heavenly View Ranch

1. This is by no means a new practice among designers of rustic architecture. In the U.S. Department of the Interior National Park Service's 1938 handbook, *Park and Recreation Structures, Part I,* architect Albert H. Good comments specifically on page 5 of "Administration and Basic Service Facilities" about "proper scale," suggesting: "In high, mountainous and forested regions the various structural elements of rustic construction—logs, timbers, rocks—must be reasonably overscaled to the structure itself to avoid being unreasonably underscaled to surrounding large trees and rough terrain. In less rugged natural areas, the style may be employed with less emphasis on oversizing."

2. As opposed to the decidedly more refined square-hewn log construction common in locations such as Virginia and throughout Russia and countries of eastern and central Europe and Scandinavia.

3. Peter Arnell and Ted Bickford, eds., *Robert A.M. Stern 1965–80: Toward a Modern Architecture after Modernism* (New York: Rizzoli, 1981): 11.

4. Albert H. Good, *Park and Recreation Structures, Part III: Overnight and Organized Camp Facilities,* reprint ed. (New York: Princeton Architectural Press, 1999): 58.

Zajac House

1. Piton is well aware of the architecture of American Henry Hobson Richardson (1838–1886), as became clear in our interview at Zajac House.

Midnight Canyon Ranch

1. See Albert H. Good, *Park and Recreation Structures,* reprint ed. (New York: Princeton Architectural Press, 1999): 29.

2. For more on Big Trees Lodge and other National Park buildings, see Good, *Park and Recreation Structures* (1999).

3. For more on Kamp Kill Kare, see Craig Gilborn, *Adirondack Camps: Homes Away from Home, 1850–1950* (Syracuse: Adirondack Museum/Syracuse University Press, 2000): 276.

Lanzinger House

1. At Lanzinger House, an overhang, or cantilever in the log course, protects the front entry. This part of the design required the installation of 3/4-inch steel rods, each several feet long, which extend vertically through holes bored into the stacked logs and can be adjusted to maintain the log compression that is inherent elsewhere in the construction. As applied here, this is an innovation.

2. Daniel Fugenschuh, "View from Innsbruck," *The Architectural Review,* vol. 214, (October 2003): 36–37.

Savage House

1. Author telephone interview with Kurt Dubbe, January 2006.

2. Originally published in Deb Barracato, "Unexpected Encore," *Teton Home* (spring/summer 2004): 43.

3. Ibid.

4. Terry G. Jordan, et al., *The Mountain West: Interpreting the Folk Landscape* (Baltimore and London: Johns Hopkins University Press, 1997): 60.

Orcas House

1. Author telephone interview with homeowner, December 2005.

2. Author interview via e-mail with Mira Jean Steinbrecher, December 2005.

3. http://www.uniquetimber.com

4. Author interview via e-mail with Mira Jean Steinbrecher, December 2005.

Draper Cabin

1. See Scully House in William Morgan, *The Abrams Guide to American House Styles* (New York: Harry N. Abrams, 2004): 411.

2. Ibid., p. 400.

3. Author telephone interview with Dan Scully, December 2005.

BIBLIOGRAPHY

Adam, Peter. *Eileen Gray: Architect, Designer*. New York: Abrams, 1987.

Aldrich, Chilson D. *The Real Log Cabin*. New York: Macmillan, 1928.

Andersson, Henrik O., and Fredric Bedoire. *Swedish Architecture: Drawings 1640–1970*. Stockholm: Byggforlaget, 1986.

Arnell, Peter, and Ted Bickford, eds. *Robert A.M. Stern 1965–80: Toward a Modern Architecture after Modernism*. New York: Rizzoli, 1981.

Barracato, Deb. "Unexpected Encore," *Teton Home* (Spring/Summer 2004): 43.

Benjamin, Susan S., ed. *An Architectural Album: Chicago's North Shore*. Winnetka: Junior League of Evanston-North Shore, 1988.

Boesiger, Willy, and Hans Girsberger. *Le Corbusier: 1910–65*. Basel: 1967.

Bradley, Robert L. *Maine's First Buildings: The Architecture of Settlement, 1604–1700*. Augusta, Maine: Maine Historic Preservation Commission, 1978.

Brittingham, John C. "Historic Houses: Neutra in Montana," *Architectural Digest* 61, no. 6 (June 2004): 50–54.

Brooks, H. Allen. *The Prairie School: Frank Lloyd Wright and His Midwest Contemporaries*. Toronto: University of Toronto Press, 1972.

Brumfield, William Craft. *A History of Russian Architecture*. New York: Cambridge University Press, 1993.

Bugge, Gunnar, and Christian Norberg-Schulz. *Early Wooden Architecture in Norway*. Oslo: Norsk Arkitekturforlag, 1990.

Calder Loth, ed. *The Virginia Landmarks Register*. 4th ed., Charlottesville: University Press of Virginia, 1999.

Chiambretto, Bruno. *Le Corbusier à Cap-Martin*. Marseille: Editions Parenthèses, 1987.

Comstock, William Phillips. *Bungalows, Camps, and Mountain Houses*. Washington, D.C.: AIA Press, 1990.

Cook, Kathleen (translator). *North Russian Architecture*. USSR: Progress, 1972.

Curtis, William J. *Modern Architecture Since 1900*. London: Phaidon Press, 1982.

Dale, Edward Everett. *Frontier Ways: Sketches of Life in the Old West*. Austin: University of Texas Press, 1959.

Davey, Peter. *Peter Zumthor: Carlsberg Architecture Prize 1998*. Copenhagen: Carlsberg, 1998.

Dietrichson, L., and H. Munthe, *Die Holzbaukunst Norwegens*. Dresden: 1893.

Domus (September 1995).

Editors of International Architecture Review, *Building in the Mountains: Recent Architecture in Graubunden*. Barcelona: G. Gili, 2000.

Eliassen, George. *Norwegian Architecture throughout the Ages*. Oslo: H. Aschehoug, 1950.

Escher, Frank, ed. *John Lautner, Architect*. New York: Princeton Architectural Press, 1998.

Floyd, Margaret Henderson. *Henry Hobson Richardson: A Genius for Architecture*. New York: Monacelli Press, 1997.

Frampton, Kenneth. *Le Corbusier: Architect of the Twentieth Century*. New York: Abrams, 2002.

Fugenschuh, Daniel. "View from Innsbruck," *The Architectural Review* 214 (October 2003): 36–37.

Futagawa, Yukio, *GA Houses 83*, Tokyo: Futagawa, 2004.

Gebhard, David. *Schindler*. San Francisco: William Stout Publishers, 1997.

Gilborn, Craig. *Adirondack Camps: Homes Away from Home, 1850–1950*. Syracuse: Adirondack Museum/Syracuse University Press, 2000.

———. *Adirondack Furniture and the Rustic Tradition*. New York: Abrams, 1987.

Goldberger, Paul. "Swiss Mystique," *Vanity Fair* (July 2001): 108–15.

Good, Albert H. *Park and Recreation Structures*. New York: Princeton Architectural Press, 1999.

Grattan, Virginia L. *Mary Colter: Builder upon the Red Earth*. Flagstaff: Northland Press, 1980.

Gronvold, Ulf. *A History of Buildings: 1,000 Years of Norwegian Architecture*. Oslo: unknown, 1997.

Guyer, I. D. *History of Chicago: Its Commercial and Manufacturing Interests and Industry*. Chicago: Church, Goodman & Cushing, 1862.

Harris, Eliza Scott. "Call of the Wild," *Departures.com*, September 2002, http://www.departures.com/tr/tr_0902_adirondacks.html.

Hassrick, Peter H. *Charles M. Russell*. New York: Abrams, 1989.

Hauglid, Roar. *Old Art and Monumental Buildings in Norway Restored During the Last Fifty Years*. Oslo: Dreyer, 1963.

Henderson, Justin. *Roland Terry: Master Northwest Architect*. Seattle and London: University of Washington Press, 2000.

Hess, Alan. *The Architecture of John Lautner*. New York: Rizzoli International Publications, 1999.

Hewitt, Mark Alan. *Gustav Stickley's Craftsman Farms: The Quest for an Arts and Crafts Utopia*. Syracuse: Syracuse University Press, 2001.

Hines, Thomas S. *Richard Neutra and the Search for Modern Architecture*. Berkeley and Los Angeles: University of California Press, 1982.

Historic American Buildings Survey, Library of Congress, Washington, D.C.

Hotaling, Mary B. "Architects and Builders of the Adirondacks," *Adirondack Architectural Heritage Newsletter* 1, no. 1 (Spring 1992): 5–8.

Hotaling, Mary B. "Framing a Legacy: How a Century-Old Firm Defined the Regional Style," *Adirondack Life* (March/April 1997): 33–39.

Jordan, Terry G. *Texas Log Buildings: A Folk Architecture*. Austin: University of Texas Press, 1978.

Jordan, Terry G., et al. *The Mountain West: Interpreting the Folk Landscape*. Baltimore and London: Johns Hopkins University Press, 1997.

Kaiser, Harvey H. *Great Camps of the Adirondacks*. Boston: David R. Godine, 1982.

Kalman, Harold. *A History of Canadian Architecture*, vol. 1. New York: Oxford University Press, 2006.

Kawashima, Chuji. *Japan's Folk Architecture: Traditional Thatched Farmhouses*. New York: Kodansha International, 1986.

Komonen, Markku. *Saarinen*. Helsinki: Museum of Finnish Architecture, 1984.

Kostrowicka, Irena. *Poland: Landscape and Architecture*. Warsaw: Arkady, 1980.

Lahti, Markku. "Alvar Aalto and the Beauty of the House." In *Alvar Aalto: Towards a Human Modernism*. Munich, London, and New York: Prestel Verlag, 1999.

Lamprecht, Barbara Mac. *Richard Neutra: The Complete Works*. Cologne: Taschen, 2000.

Lane, Barbara Miller. *National Romanticism and Modern Architecture in Germany and the Scandinavian Countries*. Cambridge: Cambridge University Press, 2000.

Loos, Adolf. "Architektur," *Der Sturm* (1910).

Macomber, Ben. *The Jewel City*. San Francisco: John J. Newbegin, 1915.

Maddex, Diane, and Alexander Vertikoff. *Bungalow Nation*. New York: Abrams, 2003.

Matthews, Henry C. *Kirtland Cutter: Architect in the Land of Promise* (Seattle: University of Washington Press, 1999.

McClelland, Linda Flint. *Building the National Parks: Historic Landscape Design and Construction*. Baltimore and London: Johns Hopkins University Press, 1998.

McCoy, Esther. *Five California Architects*. New York: Reinhold, 1960.

Menin, Sarah, and Flora Samuel. *Nature and Space: Aalto and Le Corbusier*. London and New York: Routledge, 2003.

Moller, Svend Erik. *Modern Danish Summer Bungalows*. Copenhagen: Host & Sons Forlag, 1957.

Mooslechner, Walter. *Winterholz*. Salzburg: Verlag Anton Pustet, 1997.

Morgan, William. *The Abrams Guide to American House Styles*. New York: Abrams, 2004.

Mozdzierz, Zbigniew. *The House under the Firs: The Pawlikowski Family Residence*. Zakopane: Doctor Tytus Chalubinski Tatra Museum, 2003.

Münz, Ludwig. *Adolf Loos: Pioneer of Modern Architecture*. New York: Praeger, 1966.

Neutra, Richard. *Richard Neutra on Building: Mystery and Realities of the Site*. Scarsdale, N.Y.: Morgan & Morgan, 1951.

Norberg-Schulz, Christian. "Munthe, Holm" Grove Art Online. Oxford University Press, August 10, 2005; http://www.groveart.com.ezproxy.lapl.org/.

Norberg-Schulz, Christian. *Nightlands: Nordic Building*. Cambridge and London: MIT Press, 1996.

Norri, Marja-Ritta. *Suomi Rakentaa: Finland Bygger*. Helsinki: Suomen Rakennustaiteen Museo, 1981.

Norton, Frank H. *Illustrated Historical Register of the Centennial Exhibition, Philadelphia, 1876, and of the Exposition Universelle, Paris, 1878*. New York: American News Co., 1879.

Oliver, Paul, ed. *Encyclopedia of Vernacular Architecture of the World*. Cambridge: Cambridge University Press, 1997.

Opel, Adolf and Daniel. *On Architecture: Adolf Loos*. Riverside, Calif.: Ariadne Press, 2002.

Pehnt, Wolfgang, ed. *Encyclopedia of Modern Architecture*. New York: Abrams, 1964.

Pfeiffer, Bruce Brooks, ed. *Frank Lloyd Wright: His Living Voice* (Fresno: The Press at California State University, 1987.

Post, Robert C., ed., *1876: A Centennial Exhibition*. Washington, D.C.: Smithsonian Institution, 1976.

Quinn, Ruth. *Weaver of Dreams: The Life and Architecture of Robert C. Reamer*. Bozeman, Mont.: Leslie and Ruth Quinn, Publishers, 2004.

Rheims, Maurice. *The Flowering of Art Nouveau*. New York: Abrams, 1966.

Richards, J. M. *A Guide to Finnish Architecture*. London: Hugh Evelyn, 1966.

Ritter, Arno, ed. *Josef Lackner*. Salzburg, Austria: Verlag Anton Pustet, 2004.

Schildt, Göran. *Alvar Aalto: The Complete Catalogue of Architecture, Design and Art*. New York: Rizzoli, 1994.

Schoenauer, Norbert. *6,000 Years of Housing*. New York: W. W. Norton & Co., 2000.

Schwarz, Mario. "Fin-De-Siècle Country Houses at Semmering," available on the Internet at http://www.fwf.ac.at/en/finals/final.asp?L=E&F_ID=6002740&file=c:%5Cwebsite%5Csite%5Cen%5Cfinals%5CP13959E.html.

Scully, Vincent. *The Shingle Style and the Stick Style*. Rev. ed., New Haven: Yale University Press, 1971.

Sebba, Anne. *Laura Ashley: A Life by Design*. London: Weidenfeld and Nicolson, 1990.

Shurtleff, Harold R. *The Log Cabin Myth: A Study of the Early Dwellings of the English Colonists in North America*. Gloucester, Mass.: Peter Smith, 1967.

Simonnaes, Bjorn. "Lekture 9: An Attempt to be Conscious about the Architectural Revolution in these Days" (November 1981; unpublished).

Sjöberg, Lars. *The Swedish House*. New York: Monacelli Press, 2003.

Skjelde, Atle. "A Hotel in a Class of its Own," *Seasons of Norway* (Spring/Summer 2000): 46.

Sloan, Tom L. B. "The Architecture of William W. Boyington," M.A. thesis. Northwestern University, 1962.

Smith, G. E. Kidder. *Switzerland Builds: Its Modern Architecture and Native Prototypes*. New York and Stockholm: Albert Bonnier, 1950.

Smith, Mary Ann. *Gustav Stickley: The Craftsman*. New York: Dover Publications, 1983.

Soltynski, Roman. *Glimpses of Polish Architecture*. London: Standard Art Book Co.,

Steinmann, Martin. "On the Work of Peter Zumthor," *Domus* 710 (November 1989): 52–53.

Stickley, Gustav. *More Craftsman Homes*. New York: Dover Publications, 1982.

Storrer, William Allin, *The Architecture of Frank Lloyd Wright: A Complete Catalog*. 3rd ed., Chicago: University of Chicago Press, 2002.

Taideteoksena, Koti. *Hvitträsk: The Home as a Work of Art*. Helsinki: Otava Publishing Company, 2000.

Takishita, Yoshihiro. *Japanese Country Style*. New York: Kodansha International, 2002.

Tanner, Roger (trans.). *Glimpses of Sweden: Architecture and Design*. Stockholm: Sveirge Japan Gruppen, 1985.

Thiede, Arthur, and Cindy Teipner. *American Log Homes*. Layton, Utah: Gibbs Smith, 1986.

Time Magazine Archive, "Homes Inside Out," *Time* 49, no. 5, (February 3, 1947): http://www.time.com/time/archive/preview/0,10987,886332,00.html.

Tournikiotis, Panayotis. *Adolf Loos*. New York: Princeton Architectural Press, 1994.

United States Centennial Commission, International Exhibition, 1876. Washington, D.C.: Government Printing Office, 1880–84.

Upton, Dell. *Architecture of the United States*. New York: Oxford University Press, 1998.

Valonen, Niilo. *Suomen Kansanrakennukset*. Vammala, Finland: unknown, 1994.

Von Moos, Stanislaus. *New Directions in Swiss Architecture*. New York: George Braziller, 1969.

Wahlman, Lars Israel. *Verk Av L I Wahlman*. Stockholm: AB Tidskiften Byggmästaren, 1950.

Weston, Richard. *Alvar Aalto*. London: Phaidon Press, 1995.

Wilson, Richard Guy, contributor. "America's Castles: Adirondack Camps" (New York: A&E Home Video, 1995). Documentary film.

Winter, Robert, and Alexander Vertikoff. *Craftsman Style*. New York: Abrams, 2004.

Winter, Robert, ed. *Toward a Simpler Way of Life: The Arts and Crafts Architects of California*. Berkeley, Los Angeles, and London: University of California Press, 1997.

Young, Betty Lou. *Rustic Canyon and the Story of the Uplifters*. Santa Monica: Casa Vieja Press, 1975.

Zachwatowicz, Jan. *Polish Architecture*. Warsaw: Arkady, 1968.

Zukowsky, John, ed. *Chicago Architecture 1872–1922: Birth of a Metropolis*. Chicago and Munich: Art Institute of Chicago and Prestel Verlag, 1987.

Zumthor, Peter. *Peter Zumthor Works: Buildings and Projects, 1979–97*. Baden: Muller, 1998.

INDEX

Page numbers in *italics* indicate illustrations.

Aalto, Alvar, 88, 89, 90–91, *90–91*
Academy of Fine Arts, 140
Adirondack style, 8, 11, 30, *30*, *31*, 32, 34, *34*, 36, 74, 94, 96, 97, 100, *102*, *104*
Aging, of wood, 186, *186*
AIA. *See* American Institute of Architects
Alvar Aalto Museum, Jyväsklä, 88
American Institute of Architects (AIA), 34, 223
Anglo-Western Pioneer Vernacular style, 202, *202–9*
Animal hair, as insulation, 28, *28*, 90, *90*
ArchiCenter Exhibition, 108
Architecture. *See also* Construction; *individual styles*
    awards for, 138, 165, 201, 223
    cars inspiring, 218
    earthquake-resistant, 210, 213
    as high-art, 45, 86, 88, 144, 155, 167, 196
    in National Park system, 178, 179
    Nature and, 108, 111, 124, 126, 127, *127*, 132, *138*, *139*, 141, *141*, 156, 210, 213
    organic, 183
    rustic, 178, 204
    rustic modernism in, 108, 111
Art. *See also* Arts and Crafts Movement
    craftsmanship and, 66
    high/fine, 20, 45, 86, 88, 144, 155, 167, 196
    home as total work of, 58
    Witkiewicz and fine, 45
Artek, 88
Art Nouveau, *44*, 45
Arts and Crafts Movement, 45, 60, 64, 66, 82
Ashley, David, 150, *151–55*, *153–55*
Ashley House, 150, *151–55*, *153–55*
Assembly line, 144, 156
Awards, architecture, 138, 165, 201, 223

Barberis, Charles, 116, *117–23*, 119
Barfrostue, 12, *12*
Bartusiow, Jan Obrochta, 40, *40–47*, *42*, *43*, 45, *46*
Beaux-Arts Classicism, 16
Beverly Shores, Indiana, 20
Blue Mounds, Wisconsin, 20, *20*
Boyington, William W., 30, *30–31*, *33–34*, *34*
Bozeman, Montana, 108, *109–15*, *111*, *113–14*
Branches/roots, 32, 34
Branch, William, 124, *125*, 126–28, *127–28*
Brekke, Ingeborg, 138, *139*
Brekke, Norway, 5, *5*, 138, *139–43*, *140–43*
Brekkestranda Fjord Hotel, 5, *5*, 138, *139–43*, *140–43*
Bright Angel Lodge, 10, *10*
Bristol Design Group, *214*, *216–17*

Brixlegg, Austria, 196, *197–201*, *199–201*
Bull Head Lodge, 9
Bungalow, 72, *73–79*, *75*, 82
Bungalow Bed and Breakfast, 76

Cabin. *See* Log cabin
Camp Pine Knot, 8, 32, 102
Camp Wonundra, 100, *100–107*, *102*, *104*, 107
Carchitecture, 218
Carvings, 43, 46, *46*, 61, *61*, 185
    as window treatment, 62, *62*
Central Park, New York, 18
Century of Progress Exposition, 20, 21, *21*
Chandelier, Heineman's, 96, *97*
Chemosphere House, 124, *125*, 127–28
Chicago Architecture Foundation, 108
Chicago World's Fair, 19, *19*, 20, *20*
Chinking, *33*, 79, *79*
    latex for, 32, 158, *158*
Chocholow, Poland, 15, *15*
Church(es)
    Engelbrekt, 58
    Norway's stave, 27
    Norwegian stave, 20, *20*
Church of Transfiguration of the Savior, 12, *13*
Cladding, 92, 100, 113, 119, 123, *123*
    milled-lumber frame, 220
    peeled-log, 138, *142*, *143*
    steel/log, 223
Clubhouse, Stickley Museum, 64, *65–71*, *66*, *68*, *71*
C. M. Russell Museum, 8, *8*
Coles County, Illinois, 10
Construction. *See also* Hewing; Joinery; Timber
    assembly-line, 144, 156
    chinking in, 32, *33*, 79, *79*
    cladding in, 92, 100, 113, 119, 123, *123*, 138, *142*, *143*
    exposed log, 64, 70, *71*, 72, 73–74, *74*, 76, *76*, 88, *88*, 138, *142*, *143*, 155, *155*, 180, *181*
    full log, 35
    half-timbering, 72, *73*
    horizontal log, 16, *18*
    hybrid, 178
    knitted/strickbau, 162
    masonry, 58
    milled ends in, 181
    notched log, 27, 90, *90*, 146, *146*, 162, 171, *171*, *193*, 193
    organic materials in, 171
    plain sawn, 119, *119*
    refined log, 20, *20*
    round-ended log, 102, *102*, 146, *146*

rustic log, 20, 21, *21*, 98, *98–99*, 154, 204
    salvaged material in, 153, *153*, 155, *155*, 202, *202*, 204, 207, *214*, *215*
    stave/horizontal, 16, *17*
    in United States, 8, 205
Conzett, Jürg, 162
Cottage prototype, 15, *15*, 43
    farmhouse with, 12, *12*
"The Courtship of Miles Standish" (Longfellow), 92
Cowboy artist, 8, *8*
Craftsman Farms, 64
Craftsman Home Builders Club, 64
Craftsman Movement, 9, 80
Craftsmanship. *See also* Art
    art and, 66
    European superiority of, 7–8
    innovative, 153
    Norwegian, 24, 153
    in World's Columbian Exposition, 16
Craftsman style, 11, 64, *65–71*, *66*, *68*, *71*, 72, *73–79*, 80, *81–82*, *82*, 92, *93–99*, *211–17*
Cupolas, 12, *13*
Cutter and Poetz Architects, 16
Cutter, Kirtland, 16, *19*
Cypress Log Cabin, 20, 21, *21*

Dadaist pattern, 155, *155*
Dalecarlia, 56, 60, *61*
Deconstructivism, *219–25*
Decoration
    baroque window, 15, *15*
    exposed logs as, 72, *73*
    sheepskin, 186, *187*
Deming, Washington, 156, *157–61*, 158
Distin, William G., 100, *100–107*, *102*, *104*, 107
Dom Pod Jedlami, 40, *40–47*, *42*, *43*, 45, *46*
Donovan & Rhoads, 75
Donovan, William E., *73–79*, *75*
Door
    Dutch, 96, *96*, 104, *104*
    plank, 60, *60*
    reclaimed barn, 155
Door handle, distinctive, 58, *58*, 60, *60*
Double-house, 12, *12*
Dover Neck, New Hampshire, 7
Downing, Andrew Jackson, 16
Dragon style, 24, *25*, 26, *26*, 27, *27*, 28
Drains, chain-link, *212*, 213
Draper Cabin, 218, *219–25*, *220*, *222–24*
Driftwood, 132, *133–34*, *134*
Driggs, Idaho, 202, *202–9*, *204–5*, *207*, *209*

Dubbe, Kurt, *202–9, 204*
Dubbe Moulder Architects, 204
Durant, William West, 8, 32, 100, 102
Dynamite, 154

Earthquake, design and, 210, 213
Einstein, Albert, 119
Eliassen, Georg, 22
Eliot, Maine, 7
Ends, milled log, 181
Energy efficiency, 193
Engelbrekt Church, 58
England, 8
Expositions
    Century of Progress, 20, 21, *21*
    Pan Pacific, 20, 21, 84
    Paris Universelle, 16, 20, *20*
    Philadelphia Centennial, 16, *18*, 19
    World's Columbian, 16

Faloon, Kelly F., *187–95, 188, 191, 193–94*
    energy efficiency and, 193
Farmhouse(s). *See also* Craftsman Farms
    15th century, 16, *17*
    Barfro-cottage, 12, *12*
    Finnish, 88
    Swedish, 16, *17*, 56, 60, 61
    Swedish Vernacular-style, 168, *169–75, 171, 174*
Farmhouse Vernacular/Strickbau, 162, *163–67, 165, 167*
Fenestration, landscape and, 29, *29*, 119, 199
Fine Art. *See* High-art
Finnish National Museum, 51
Finnish National Romantic style, 48, *49–50*, 51, *53*
Flexihouse, 140
Floorboards, distressed, *194, 194*
Flying saucer, on logs, *124, 125*
Foundation
    dynamite for preparing, 154
    granite, 48, *49*
    native/local stone, *142, 143*, 154, 185
    Neo-Romanesque stone, 42, *42, 43*
Frögnerseteren, *1, 5, 24, 25–29, 27–29*
Frost Garrison, 7

Gesellius, Herman, 48, *49–50*, 51, *52–55, 53*
Gesellius, Lindren, and Saarinen (GLS), 51
Glacier National Park, 9, 19
Glass, inserted into logs, *128, 128*
GLS. *See* Gesellius, Lindren, and Saarinen
Golden Section, 119
Gold Hill, Colorado, 150, *151–55, 153–55*
Gothic, 34
Grand Canyon National Park, 10
Grand Teton, 204
Granite, 48, *49*
Great Camp, 100, 102
Great Falls, Montana, *8, 8*
Gugalun, 7, 162, *163–67, 165, 167*

Hallingdal, Norway, 14, *14*
Halvorsgard Lofthouse, 14, *14*
Hancock, New Hampshire, 218, *219–25*
Hansteen, Waldemar, *20, 20*
Heavenly View Ranch, *176, 177, 178, 179–81, 181*
Heimatstil, 80, *81–82, 82, 83, 83*
Heineman, Alfred, 92, *93–99, 94, 96, 98*
Heineman, Arthur, 92
Helburn House, 108, *109–15, 111, 113–14*
Helburn, Nicholas, 113
Hellman House, 92, *93–99, 94, 96, 98*
Helsinki Railway Station, 51
Hetherington, Murray D., 20, 21, *21*
Hewing
    end-only, *191, 193*
    rough, 34, *35*, 38, *38*, 43
    square, 7, *7*, 12, *12*, 45, *45*, 196, 205
Hexagon, 144, *145*
Highland Park, Illinois, 30, *30, 31*
Hindry House, 92, 94
Historicism, Modernism and, 199
History, accuracy in, 204
Homeland style, 80, *81–82, 82, 83, 83*
Hotel(s)
    Brekkestranda Fjord, *5, 5*, 138, *139–43, 140–43*
    Bungalow Bed and Breakfast, 76
    Old Faithful Inn, 9, 76
    The Point, *100–107, 102, 104, 107*
House of Hoo-Hoo, *20–21, 21*
HP Woodworking, *202–9, 204*
Hvitträsk, 48, *49–50*, 51, *52–55, 53, 54*
    museum, 54

Idaho State Building, 19, *19*
Idylwild, California, *124, 125, 126–28, 127–28*
Illinois State Building, 34
Image. *See* Perceptions
Indian Dunes National Lakeshore, 20
Insulation
    animal hair, 28, *28*, 90, *90*
    latex, *158, 158*
    newspaper, 204
    wood shavings as, *45, 45*
    wool, *102, 102*

Jackson Park, Chicago, 16
Jefferson, Thomas, tiles of, *150, 151*
John F. Kennedy International Airport, 54
Joinery, *226–27*
    dovetail/half-dovetail, 168, 206
    full-scribe, 28, *28*, 61, *61*, 146, *146*
    in rectangle v. other construction, 156
    tooth-notch, 90, *90*

The Kalevala, 48
Karelia, 48
Karelian prototype, 48, 51
Karstula, Finland, 88, *89*, 90–91, *90–91*
The Khuner House, *83, 83*

Kiln, drying, 213
Kirkkonummi, Finland, 48, *49–50*, 51, *52–55, 53–54*
Kizhi Island museum, 15, *15*
Kizhi Island, Russia, 12, *13*
Knutsen, Knut, 138
Koether House, 144, *145–49, 146, 149*
Koether, Walter, 144, 146
Kölbel, Katharina, 146, *147, 148*
Kootenai Lodge, 19
Koshel house prototype, 15, *15*

Lake McDonald, Montana, *9, 9*
Lake Onega, Russia, 12, *13*
Landmark. *See* National Historic Landmark
Landscape, *212, 213*
    fenestration and, 29, *29*, 119, 199
Landström, Anders, 168, *169–75*
Lanzinger, Antonius, 196, *197–201, 199–201*
Lanzinger House, 196, *197–201, 199–201*
Latex, 32, *158, 158*
Lautner, John, Wright and, 124
Le Corbusier, 88, 116, *117–23, 119–21, 123*
    Golden Section used by, 119
    murals of, 116, 121, *121*
Le Modulor, 116, 119
Le Petit Cabanon, 116, *117–23, 119*, 121, 123
Letters, between architect and owner, 72, *75, 75*
Lincoln, Abraham, *10, 10*
Lincoln Logs, 6
Lindgren, Armas, 48, *49–50*, 51, *52–55, 53*, 88
Lindroos, Hjalmar, 48, *49–50, 52–55*
Linstow, H.D.F., 27
Little Norway, *20, 20*
Lodge(s), 19
    Bright Angel, *10, 10*
    Bull Head, 9
    Kootenai, 19
    in National Park system, 178, *179*
Loft house prototype, 14, *14*, 56
Log(s). *See also* Timber
    chestnut, 64
    cladding of, 92, 100, 113, 119, 123, *123*, 138, *142, 143*, 220, 223
    corbelled, 16, *18*, 19, *19*, 27, 56, *56*, 126, *126*, 215
    dead, *153, 153*
    double/locked-tooth, 162
    dressing up, 90
    driftwood, 132, *133–34, 134*
    end-only hewing, *191, 193*
    eucalyptus, *96, 97*
    exposed, 64, 70, *71*, 72, *73–74, 74*, 76, *76*, 88, *88*, 138, *142, 143*, 155, *155*, 180, *181*
    flying saucer on, *124, 125*
    glass inserted into, *128, 128*
    knitted, 162
    plain sawn, 119, *119*
    rough-hewn, 34, *35*, 38, *38*, 43
    round-ended, *102, 102*, 146, *146*
    saddle-notched, 146, *146*, 193, *193*

shortage of, 100
shrinkage of, *148*, 149, 158, 183, 213
square-hewn, 7, *7*, 12, *12*, 45, *45*, 196, 205
tooth-notched, 90, *90*, 171, *171*
vacuum-kiln drying of, 213
Log cabin. *See also* Log House(s)
American image of, 10
American, v. European log house, 6, 7, 12, 144
myth, 65
National Park Service and, 10
perceptions of, 6, 8, 9, 10, 64, 220
pioneer, 178
U.S. Presidents and, 6
Log House, 84, *85*, 86, *87*
Log house(s)
European, v. American log cabin, 6, 7, 12, 144
Lautner family, 126, *126*
oldest U.S., 12, *12*
in world fairs, 19–20, *19–20*
Loos, Adolf, 80, *81–83*, *82–83*
Loos Haus Restaurant, 83, *83*
Lopez Island, Washington, 130, *130*, *131*, 132,
133–37, *134*, 137
Lumber. *See* Timber

Marionette Theater, *18*, 19
Marshall Field & Company, 76, *78*, 78
Masonry construction, 58
Materials, organic, 171
Maushak, Jim, *157–61*, 158
Maybeck, Bernard, 20, 21, *21*
Mediterranean Sea, 119
Midnight Canyon Ranch, *187–95*, *188*, 191, *198–94*
Millard Park, 32
Miller Lane, Barbara, 24, 58, 168
Mississippi State Building, *18*, 19
Mississippi Valley Industrial, *18*, 19
Modernism, 86, 88
high-art, 196
historicism and, 199
rustic, 108, 111
Modern style, 11, 83, *83*, 108, 111, 113, 196, 199. *See
also* Pacific Northwest Modern
Montana, *187–95*, *188*, 191, *193–94*
Morris Plains, New Jersey, 64, *65–71*, 66, 68, 71
Morton Homestead, 12, *12*
Motif, highlander, 185
Movement(s)
Arts and Crafts, 45, 60, 64, 66, 82
Craftsman, 9, 80
National Romantic, 11
Movie set, Hellman House as, 92
Müller, Beat, 165
Munthe, Holm Hansen, *1*, 5, 24, *26*, 27, *27*, 28, *28*,
29, *29*
Münz, Ludwig, 80, *81–82*
Murals, of Le Corbusier, 116, 121, *121*
Museum(s)
Alvar Aalto, 88

C.M. Russell, 8, *8*
Finnish National, 51
Hvitträsk as, 54
Kizhi Island, 15, *15*
Norsk Folk-, 14, *14*, 27
Stickley Clubhouse, 64, *65–71*, 66, 68, 71
Tatra, 43
Villa Koliba, 42

National Historic Landmark
Power House as, 76
Stickley Museum as, 66
Nationalism
American, 66
Finnish, 48
Munthe's contribution to Norway's, 27
Polish, 43
Swedish, 60
National monument, Dom Pod Jedlami as, 45
National Parks Service, 32
Cypress Log Cabin and, 20
lodge architecture in, 178, *179*
recreational log cabin and, 10
National Park Vernacular, *187–95*, *188*, 191, *193–94*
National Register for Historic Places, 9, 20, 36
Nature, architecture and, 108, 111, 124, 126, 127,
127, 132, 138, *139*, 141, *141*, 156, 210, 213
Navajo Indians, hexagon use of, 144
Needham Construction, 210
Neiman, David, as architect/builder, 158
Neutra, Richard, 108, *109–15*, 111, *113–14*
New England, 7
Newspaper, for insulation, 204
New Sweden colony, 12, *12*
Nieman Guest House, 156, *157–61*, 158, 160
Nordic Classicism, 88, 90
Norsk Folkmuseum, 14, *14*, 27
Norway, farms of, 12
Notching, 27
double/locked-tooth, 162
saddle, 146, *146*
tooth, 90, *90*, 171, *171*

Okanogan Contemporary style, 144, *145–49*, 146,
149
Old Faithful Inn, 9, 76
Orcas House, 210, *211–17*, 213, *215*
Orcas Island, Washington, 210, *211–17*, 213, *215*
Organic style, 124, 127, *127–28*, 128, 130, *131*, 132,
138, *139* 141, *141*
Ornamentation, 80, 83, *83*, 90, *91*. *See also*
Decoration
branches/roots for, 32, 34
carved, 43, 45, 46, *46*, 61, *61*, 185
Dadaist floor, 155, *155*
jigsaw-cut, *44*, 45
ridge-beam, 51, *52*
Ornässtuga, 16, *17*
Oshevnev House, 15, *15*

Oshevnevo, Russia, 15, *15*
Oslofjorden, Frögnerseteren overlooking, *29*
Oslo, Norway, *1*, 5, 24, *25*, *26*, 27, *27*, 28
OSR. *See* Ottenheimer, Stern, and Reichel
Osterdal, Norway, 12, *12*
Ottenheimer, Stern, and Reichel (OSR), 84

Pacific Lumbermen's Association, 20
Pacific Northwest Modern, 130, *130*, *131*, 132,
133–37, *134*, 137
Pacific Northwest Rural Vernacular, 156, *157–61*,
158, 160
Paint, tooth notching and, 171, *171*
Pan Pacific Exposition, San Francisco, 20, 21, 84
Parallelograms, 218, 220
Paris Exposition Universelle of 1900, 16, 20, *20*
Parstuga, 12, *12*
Partitioning, adjustable room, 174, *174*
Pauroso, Dan, *202–9*
Pavilion Hans Haugens, 28
Pearlman Cabin, 124, *125*, 126–28, *127–28*
Perceptions
of log cabin, 6, 8, 9, 10, 64, 220
Shurtleff's log cabin myth and, 65
Philadelphia Centennial Exposition, 16, *18*, 19
Piazza, 64, 65
Piers, stone, 76, *76*
Pisciotta, Richard, *219–25*
Piton, Sebastian, 182, *183–87*, 185, 186
Witkiewicz and, 183
The Point, 100, *100–107*, 102, *104*, 107
Polytechnic Institute, Helsinki, 48
Porch. *see* Piazza
Power, Charles B., Reamer and, 72, 75, *75*
Power House, 72, *73–79*, *74–76*, 79
Prairie style, 11, 84, *85*, 86, *87*
Prefabrication, 168, *169–75*
Prospect Park, Pennsylvania, 8
Prototypes
cottage, 15, *15*, 43
double-house, 12, *12*
Karelian, 48, 51
loft-house, 14, *14*, 56
Russian/Koshel, 15, *15*

Queen Anne style, 40

Ravine Beach, 32
Ravine Lodge, 30, *31*, 32, *33–39*, 34, 36, 38
Reamer, Robert C., 8–9, 32, 72, 74, 75, 76
letter to Power from, 72, 75, *75*
Rectangle, joinery for, 156
Renaissance style, 90, *90*
Restoration, 45, 72, *73*, 76, *164*, 165, 167, *167*
Ridge-beam, as ornament, 51, *52*
Rockefeller, William Avery, 100, 102
Rohe, Mies van der, 88
Romanticism, 11
in Finland, 51

in Poland, 43
in Sweden, 58, 168
Romantic Movement, 11
Rooms, adjustable, 174, *174*
Roots/branches, as ornamentation, 32, 34
Roquebrune-Cap-Martin, France, 116, *117–23*, 119, 121, 123
Royal Institute of Technology, Stockholm, 58
"Rules for Building in the Mountains" (Loos), 83
Russell, Charles M., 8, *8*, 9, *9*

Saarinen, Eliel, 48, *49–50*, 51, *52–55*, 53, 54
Salvage, 153, *153*, 155, *155*, 202, *202*, 204, 207, 214, 215
Sandell, Thomas, 168, *169–75*
San Francisco, California, 20, 21, *21*
Santa Monica, California, 92, *93–99*, 94, 96, 98
Saranac Lake, New York. *See* Upper Saranac Lake
Sauna buildings, 88
Savage House, 202, *202–9*, *204–5*, 207, 209
Schindler-Chase House, 86
Schindler, Rudolf M., Wright and, 86
Screw jacks, 183
Scully, Daniel Vincent, 218, *219–25*, 220, *222–24*
Scully, Vincent, 27, 225
Semmering, Austria, 80, *81–82*, 82–83, *83*
Semmering House, 80, *81–82*, 82–83
Settlement. *See* Shrinkage
Shavings. *See* Wood
Sheepskin, 186, *187*
Shrinkage, *148*, 149, 158, 183, 213
Shure, Ed, *151–55*, 153–54
Shurtleff, Harold R., 66
Simonnaes, Bjorn, 5, *5*, 138, *139*, *140–43*, 140–43
Wright and, 138
Smash Design, 207, *207*
Snowmass, Colorado, 176, *177*, 178, *179–81*, 181
Sonck, Lars, 48
Steinbrecher, Mira Jean, 210, *211–17*, 213
Stern, Robert A. M., 176, *177*, 178, *179–81*, 181
Stetten, Germany, 144, *145–49*, 146, 149
Stickley, Gustav, 64, *65–71*, 66, 68, 71, 82
Stickley Museum Clubhouse, 64, *65–71*, 66, 68, 71
Stocksund, Sweden, 56, *56*, *57–63*, 58, *60–63*
Stone
foundation, Neo-Romansesque, 42, *42*, 43
indigenous, 132, *142*, 143, 185
piers, 76, *76*
Studio House, Zumthor's award-winning, 165
Style. *See individual styles*
Swedish Farmhouse Vernacular, 168, *169–75*, 171, 174
Swedish Schoolhouse, 16, *18*
Swiss chalet, 19, *19*
Swiss/stick, 24, 27
Swiss Village, 20, *20*

Tallom, 56, *56*, *57–63*, 58, *60–63*
Tatra Mountains, 42, 45, 185
Tatra Museum, 43

Technical School, Dresden, Germany, 80
Telemark, Norway. *See* Norsk Folkmuseum
Terry House, 130, *130*, *131*, 132, *133–37*, 134, 137
Terry, Roland, 130, *130*, *131*, 132, *133–37*, 134, 137
Tiles, Jefferson's, 150, *151*
Timber
chestnut, 64
Douglas fir, 144, *145*
elm, 36, *37*
eucalyptus, 96, 97
indigenous, 132
Mississippi, 18
pine, 12, 13, 88, 102, *102*
salvaged, 153, *153*, 155, *155*, 202, *202*, 204, 207, *214*, 215
shortage of, 100
Torö, Sweden, 168, *169–75*
Tower, shape of Lanzinger House, *197–98*, 199
Tradition, 7
Train, building in shape of, 218
Tryvann Hill, 27
Tunebjer House "Vistet," 168, *169–75*, 171, 174
Tveito Loft, 14, *14*

Unique Timber, 213
United States
Arts and Crafts Movement in, 64, 66
construction in, 8, 205
log cabin image in, 10
log cabin v. European log house, 6, 7, 12, 144
nationalism in, 66
oldest log houses in, 12, *12*
Upper Saranac Lake, New York, 100, *100–107*, 102, 104, 107

Versam, Switzerland, 162, *163–67*, 165, 167
Villa Koliba, 42
Villa Vekara, 88, 89, *90–91*, 90–91
Vogel, Zeno, 165

Wagner, Richard, 45
Wahlman, Lars Israel, 56, *56*, *57–63*, 58, *60–63*
Water Works Tower, 34
Welsh Farmhouse Vernacular, *151–55*
White City style, 16
Wilhelm II, Emperor, 28
William Buckey O'Neill Cabin, 11, *11*
William Damm Garrison, 7, *7*
Wilson, Woodrow, 10
Window(s). *See also* Fenestration
early houses without, 14
treatment, 15, *15*, 62, *62*
Witkiewicz, Stanislaw, 40, *40–47*, 42, 43, 45, 46, 183, 185
Wolf Creek, Montana, 72, *73–79*, *74–76*, 79
Wood
aging of, 186, *186*
shavings, for insulation, 45, *45*
shavings in Zakopane style, 186, *186*

Woodman Institute, 7
Wood Prize, 138
Wool, as insulation, 102, *102*
World Fair, Chicago's, 19, *19*
World's Columbian Exposition, 16
Wright, Frank Lloyd, 84, 86, 124, 138, 144

Yellowstone National Park, 9, 32, 191
Yellowstone Traditions, *187–95*, 188

Zajac House, 182, *183–87*, 185–86
Zakopane, Poland, 40, *40–47*, 42, 43, 45–46, 182, *183–87*, 185, 186
Zakopane style, 15, 40, *40–47*, 42, 43, 45–46, 182, *183–87*
Zumthor, Peter, 162, *163–67*, 165, 167

AUTHOR'S ACKNOWLEDGMENTS

For my mother, Diane

In early 2005, photographer Radek Kurzaj and I embarked together on a thrilling international journey to locate and document architect-designed log houses for this book. The trip, made almost entirely by car, ultimately took us across the United States and through parts of Poland, Germany, Austria, Switzerland, Liechtenstein, Italy, France, the Czech Republic, the Slovak Republic, Finland, Sweden, and Norway. The logistics of determining if the houses we had heard about actually existed, in addition to learning about their current condition and exact location (some of these houses have no formal address), as well as finding owners and overcoming language barriers, required the help of a multitude of gracious individuals. Without the generous assistance of the architects, builders, and homeowners mentioned in the book, along with the many friends acknowledged below according to the countries for which they provided help, this effort would not have been possible.

Austria

Alastair Gordon

Steiner Family, Loos Haus Hotel and Restaurant

Maria Szadkowska, Villa Müller

Kurt Zweifel, ProHolz Austria

Finland

Pepita Ehrnrooth-Jokinen, Hvitträsk

Arne Heporauta, Alvar Aalto Museum Architectural Heritage

Kirsi Riihioj, the City of Kuru

Leena Strandén

France

Céline Moulard, HNA Books

Germany

Katharina Koelbel

Mira Jean Steinbrecher

Norway

Bjorn Brekke, Brekkestranda Fjord Hotel

Eileén Olstad Ree, Frognerseteren

Birgit Rusten, Norske Arkitekters Landsforbund

Poland

Zbigniew Mozdzierz

Magdalena Olsen

Wojtek Trzebunia

Sweden

Mark Bengtsson, Moderna Museet Stockholm

Ola Nilsson

Switzerland

Carla Rada, Architekturbüro Peter Zumthor

United States

Nicolette Bromberg, University of Washington Libraries

Peter Morris Dixon

Harry F. Drabik

Simon Elliott, University of California Los Angeles Libraries

Mary Supley Foxworth, Simoneink

John Graham, The Point

Mike Harding, Xanterra Parks and Resorts

Alan Hess

Mary Hotaling, Historic Saranac Lake

Arlette Klaric, The Stickley Museum at Craftsman Farms

Steve and Cindy Kleimer

Beth Ann McPherson, The Stickley Museum at
    Craftsman Farms

Ed Marquand

Dion Neutra, Richard and Dion Neutra Architects

Steve Pauly

Dan Pauroso

John Pore

Jay Pridmore

Chandler Rashley

Simone Rathlé, Simoneink

Roderick Romero

Ann Scheid, Greene and Greene Archives,
    Huntington Library

Dan Scully

Ed Shure

Paul Skinner

Bruce Smith, The Arts & Crafts Press

Cristine Wehner

Robert Winter

Randy Young, Pacific Palisades Historical Society

This book also owes much to its acquiring editor, Sigi Nacson, and HNA Books editor in chief, Eric Himmel, who recognized its potential and put their faith in us to carry it out. Thanks also go to graphic designer Brady McNamara for his sensitive approach to the material's presentation and to production manager Jane Searle for carefully directing the printing process. Lastly, I must acknowledge my overwhelming debt to the book's editor, Barbara Burn. One of the field's most talented individuals, Barbara pushed me when I needed it, and the book is immensely better for her having led the HNA team.

EDITOR: Barbara Burn
DESIGNER: Brady McNamara
LAYOUT AND COMPOSITION: Neil Egan
PRODUCTION MANAGER: Jane Searle

LIBRARY OF CONGRESS CATALOGING-IN-PUBLICATION DATA

Olsen, Richard

    Log houses of the world / by Richard Olsen ; photography by Radek Kurzaj ;
       with drawings by David Perrelli.

    p. cm.

    Includes bibliographical references and index.

    ISBN 10: 0–8109–5746–9 (hardcover)

    ISBN 13: 978–0–8109–5746–6

    1. Log cabins—Europe. 2. Log cabins—United States. I. Kurzaj, Radek, 1976–
      II. Title.

    NA8470.O47 2006

    728.3'7–dc22

              2006006423

HNA
harry n. abrams, inc.
a subsidiary of La Martinière Groupe

115 West 18th Street
New York, NY 10011
www.hnabooks.com